THE ART OF
SEAMUS HEANEY

THE ART OF
SEAMUS HEANEY

Edited & Introduced
by
Tony Curtis

POETRY WALES PRESS
DUFOUR EDITIONS
1985

Published in the United Kingdom by Poetry Wales Press
56 Parcau Avenue, Bridgend, Mid Glamorgan

First published 1982
Second edition 1985

British Library Cataloguing in Publication Data

Curtis, Tony 1946-
    The art of Seamus Heaney.
    1. Heaney—Seamus 1939-. —Criticism
    and interpretation
    I. Title
    821'.914   PR6058.E2

    U.K. ISBN 0-907476-42-2

Cover Design: Dragonfly Design

First published in the United States of America in 1985
by Dufour Editions Inc., Chester Springs, Pennsylvania 19425

Library of Congress Cataloguing-in-Publication Data
Main entry under title:

    The Art of Seamus Heaney.
    Bibliography:p.
    Includes index.
    1. Heaney, Seamus — Criticism and interpretation —
    Addresses, essays, lectures. I. Curtis, Tony,
    1946-
    PR6058.E2Z55   1985   821'.914   85-4488
    ISBN 0-8023-1279-9

Printed in 11pt Baskerville II
by
J.W. Arrowsmith Ltd.

Contents

Acknowledgements

I should like to acknowledge the help of the following in the production of this book: my publisher Cary Archard; colleagues at the Polytechnic of Wales, especially librarian Scott Robertson; Stephen Dobyns at Goddard College; Faber & Faber, Heaney's British publishers; and Seamus Heaney himself, who has observed the whole project with an entirely proper restraint.
My wife Margaret and my children Gareth and Bronwen are, as always, long suffering and supportive.

Tony Curtis

Poems and long quotations reproduced by permission of Faber & Faber Ltd., from *North, Field Work, Station Island* and *Sweeney Astray.*
In the U.S., excerpts reprinted by permission of Farrar, Straus and Giroux, Inc. from: *Poems 1965-1975,* © 1966, 1969, 1972, 1975, 1980 by Seamus Heaney. *Field Work,* © 1976, 1979 by Seamus Heaney. *Station Island,* © 1985 by Seamus Heaney. *Sweeney Astray,* © 1983 by Seamus Heaney.

The Poetry Wales Press works with the financial support of the Welsh Arts Council.

Introduction

If poetry is worth writing, and worth writing about, it has to matter, not only within the closed circle of the academy, but also in the world of telegrams and anger. It must speak to people. The most successful British poets in the last quarter of a century, those who could meaningfully claim a wide readership, a "public", have been Ted Hughes and Philip Larkin. Each of these men has a clear, distinctive voice that is accessible, that engages the reader powerfully as a contemporary.

This book seeks to illuminate the qualities of another such writer. Seamus Heaney, since the appearance of his first collection of poems in 1966, has been widely recognised as one of the most vital forces in contemporary writing on either side of the Atlantic. *The Art of Seamus Heaney* traces thematically and chronologically the development of this poet's voice since that first book, *Death of a Naturalist*. This collection of essays is formed, quite deliberately, of distinct, diverse and sometimes opposed views regarding Seamus Heaney's work. He was born in 1939 and has been publishing collections for just sixteen years. The impact which his writing has had is already significant, but these are still early days in terms of a poet's life and so one must expect critical approaches rather than absolute critical judgements. Heaney talking of Yeats has said:

> What Yeats offers the practising writer is an example of labour, perseverance. He is, indeed, the ideal example for a poet approaching middle age. He reminds you that revision and slogwork are what you may have to undergo if you seek the satisfactions of finish; he bothers you with the suggestion that if you have managed to do one kind of poem in your own way, you should cast off that way and face into another area of your experience until you have learned a new voice to say that area properly.
>
> 'Yeats as an Example?' *Preoccupations*.

Heaney is clearly structuring his own progress here.

The six writers engaged in this book are creative artists themselves: Heaney is a craftsman and naturally attracts other writers. The published poems proclaim that craft, but by including the complete drafts of the title poem of *North* I hope to illustrate the genesis and structure of Seamus Heaney's writing process, both its craft and technique. Several years ago at the Polytechnic of Wales we organised an exhibition of manuscripts from the leading poets in Wales. One writer, however, declined to participate. I received a postcard reply with the words ''The Muse is a lady and does not appear in public without her clothes.'' That is a valid line to take, but I was delighted to find Seamus Heaney taking a different one and being prepared to cooperate in this book.

As one follows the drafts of 'North' what strikes one is the sense of discipline. The poet builds on the original idea with a commitment to clarity and control. Intrigued by the central idea of place and cultural determinants, he works to define his own position, to catch feelings in the tightening net of language.

By this point, 1975, and his fourth collection, Seamus Heaney has an assured command of the poet's craft and a firm poetic stance or ''technique''. But those accomplishments were projected from his first publication. When *Death of a Naturalist* appeared from Faber & Faber in 1966 it received considerable critical acclaim:

> . . . His words give us the soil-reek of Ireland, the colourful violence of his childhood on a farm in Derry. The full-blooded energy of these poems make *Death of a Naturalist* the best first book of poems I've read for some time.'
>
> C. B. Cox in *The Spectator*

> 'What delights, in poem after poem, is the accuracy and freshness with which sense-impressions are recorded.'
>
> Richard Kell in *The Guardian*

> 'The power and precision of his best poems are a delight, and as a first collection *Death of a Naturalist* is outstanding.'
>
> Christopher Ricks in the *New Statesman*

Here was a poet who convinced one of his perception and honesty, a poet defining himself in his particular context, responding to the rural Ireland of his youth and to a deepening understanding of his heritage. He is securing that grip on his identity, and his credentials as a poet, an Irish poet, being published in London, concern him greatly at this point. He realises that "I began as a poet when my roots were crossed with my reading."

The second edition of *North* underlines the sense of that move. Heaney recognises in himself the need to escape "the tight gag of place/And time." It's as if he's bound by the pressures of events and those of the literary climate in Ulster.

> . . . of the "wee six" I sing
> Where to be saved you only must save face
> And whatever you say, you say nothing.

That poem 'Whatever you say Say Nothing' is an angry, despairing reaction against the seemingly hopeless situation in the North. But, unbearable though the pressures, political and literary, may be, the events in Ulster are "The once in-a-lifetime portent," and no artist could, or should ignore that.

Seamus Heaney's fifth collection, *Field Work* (1979), represents a move away from the mythical, historical aspects of the two previous books. "I no longer wanted a door into the dark—I want a door into the light. . . . I really wanted to come back to be able to use the first person singular to mean *me* and my lifetime." The Troubles may no longer be in the foreground of the work, but the emotional consequences of the violence are in focus. The book has a series of moving elegies, notably that for Colum McCartney, 'The Strand at Lough Beg'. This man was Heaney's cousin, a victim of a random sectarian killing in the late summer of 1975. Both he and Louis O'Neill, the victim of 'Casualty', represent all the dead of the Troubles. They are the points at which the public events, the statistics, intersect with the personal life of the poet.

In the autumn of 1984 Faber published simultaneously two new books by Heaney, *Sweeney Astray* and *Station Island*. The first of these was a poetry and prose rendition of *Buile Suibhne*, one of the earliest extant Irish works of literature and legend. Heaney fixes on the Sweeney figure and loads him with a significance, for Ireland and the Irish character, as well as for the poet's own life: "as exemplary for all men and women in contemporary Ulster", and "as an aspect of the quarrel between free creative imagination and the constraints of religious, political and domestic obligation".

The Sweeney myth also underlies several poems in *Station Island*, especially in its third section, twelve poems born of Heaney's "penance" at Station Island. Just as the pilgrims walk barefoot in circles over the rough stones of the ancient monks' cells, so the poet treads over the painful ground of his recent personal history. He encounters twelve ghosts who question his actions and the purpose of his art. These include William Carleton, the nineteenth century novelist, Patrick Kavanagh and James Joyce. It is clear that Heaney is using these visitant voices to confront the legitimacy of his art in the specific, and specifically politicised, context of Ireland. Such voices have been invoked in earlier work: from the dismissive comments of his rural ancestors to the Sybil in the 'Triptych' of *Field Work*. What is distinct in this new collection is the intensity of the concern and the serious examination of the functions his poetry performs.

Most remarkably, in the eighth of these poems, Colum McCartney re-appears to accuse the poet:

> You confused evasion and artistic tact. . .
> and saccharined my death with morning dew.

As long as Seamus Heaney remains as self-critical as that, he is surely destined to forge a poetry of considerable and lasting weight.

Fellow Irish poet, Derek Mahon, has spoken of their work in that country as ". . . an eddy of semantic scruple/in an unstructurable sea." And in glossing the final words of advice from the ghost of Joyce in poem XII of 'Station Island' the poet tells himself, "Calm down, Get back to lyric poetry. And enjoy it. You have no business setting the times wrong or right. Take pleasure." (B.B.C. Radio Four 'Kaleidoscope' Oct.1984.) Poetry from Ireland, even that of Seamus Heaney, may not affect major or immediate change in that land or beyond, but the positive values of a poetic vision as determined and honest as Heaney's are compelling. He says:

> "At one minute you are drawn towards the old vortex of racial
> and religious instinct, at another time you seek the mean of
> human love and reason."

In all his books Seamus Heaney's concern has been to draw on both these feelings. In an age which has scant regard for poetry, Heaney's work stands as a vital example of the contemporary poet's strengths and dilemmas. These essays work to understand and evaluate his unique voice, the historical, political and literary contexts in which Seamus Heaney writes, and to illuminate the poet's firm belief that "The end of Art is peace."

Tony Curtis, 1982 & 1985

ROLAND MATHIAS

Death of a Naturalist

Death of a Naturalist

When Seamus Heaney published his first volume of poetry, Ted Hughes's *The Hawk in the Rain* was nine years old and his *Lupercal* seven. It may seem no sort of praise to begin by linking Heaney with another and older writer, and yet the link has a climatic veracity about it. The civilised precisions of 'The Movement' were looking a little tired: a new force had invaded the scene and Hughes was that force. In *Lupercal* in particular he had celebrated the qualities needed for survival, whether in Dick Straightup who was chipped out of the gutter at eighty "warm as a pie and snoring" or in Esther's Tomcat who still

> Grallochs odd dogs on the quiet,
> Will take the head clean off your simple pullet,
>
> Is unkillable.

An animal dead was nothing, without dignity: but alive, if only in imagination, its peculiar spirit was trenchant, fearsome. In Hughes's 'View of a Pig' the animal dead was "Just so much/A poundage of lard and pork" but resurrected, stereotyped, he bit out his own place in the hierarchy of living:

> Pigs must have hot blood, they feel like ovens.
> Their bite is worse than a horse's—
> They chop a half-moon clean out.
> They eat cinders, dead cats.

Seamus Heaney's 'Turkeys Observed' is some way after this in force but not in concept and even his very successful and highly individual poem 'Trout' owes some of its consistent imagery of force to poems like Hughes's 'Thrushes' and 'Hawk Roosting'. Temporarily, at least, Heaney is drawn into the bruising darkness of instinct and sensation which is Hughes's world.

No good purpose is served by pressing that debt too far, because it would not be difficult to compile, even within the limits of Heaney's first book, an instant list of dissimilarities. But the point is worth making because the first third of *Death of a Naturalist*—that third which gives its distinctive character—is pretty clearly a response to the new climate in poetry initiated by Ted Hughes.

Heaney decided to invoke the atmosphere and experience of his childhood at Mossbawn between Castledawson and Toome in County Derry in language which not merely marked the muddied bucolic as a youth apart but underlined the clumsy force of that natural world with which the child had had to come to terms. Life was not merely to be caught ankle-deep in field and garden and bog, but "in the sucking clabber" of "the clods" should be made to sound like it.

There is a key of sorts to the way the poet saw this in 'Poem', subtitled 'For Marie'. In this piece to his wife (which might well have been an envoi for the book were it not displaced by a better and no less significant poem 'Personal Helicon') he writes of perfecting

> the child
> Who diligently potters in my brain
> Digging with heavy spade till sods were piled
> Or puddling through muck in a deep drain.

The world of that child, with its "bastions of clay and mush", was not merely indigenous: it was part of the poet's inheritance of touch and sound and feeling. But it was also temporary, as temporary indeed as growing away from it would make necessary. 'Poem' tells the reader that this lost bucolic world is to be perfected once before it is put away, before the poet accepts that the "new limits . . . the world/Within our walls", the world of his marriage, his teaching experience and his later life is what will matter to him in terms of feeling and inspiration from that point on.

Death of a Naturalist, then, falls into two diverging parts, the first and shorter the noisy one of childhood and youth, the second more occasional and desultory and locked into place with the first by the key poem 'Personal Helicon'. Of the two, it is the first that makes the book known, for it is in the early poems that Heaney's powers of language are employed orchestrally, with a full score for the percussion: it is in this that the texture of the writing recreates and objectifies that slow and exact rural living, that awesomely familiar existence that the poet knows he can use only once, for its own sake, before it slips away behind the increasingly intrusive bulks of time. If *Death of a Naturalist* in its most identifiable part is a trackback, it is not so because a search for origins helps to sentimentalise the writer matured. On the contrary, however much of a beginning it was, it was intended with force and awe, in the terms that Alfred Alvarez set down in his Introduction to his Penguin anthology, *The New Poetry* (1962), when he wrote that the savagery of two world wars, of concentration camps, of the human libido (as revealed in psycho-analysis) had destroyed gentility, in poetry as elsewhere:

> And gentility is a belief that life is always more or less orderly, people always more or less polite, their emotions and habits more or less decent and more or less controllable; that God, in short, is more or less good[1].

To allege this is not to infer that Heaney intended deliberately to savage or Freudianise his recollection. *Death of a Naturalist* was probably the instinctive response of a poet with a high gift of language: he knew how to create the kind of poetic texture which answered the new critical expectations.[2]

If the example of Ted Hughes was a marker for this, it is no less obvious that the momentum of Heaney's writing was very different. There is in Heaney little of that biological ferment that shivers the reader in Hughes's 'Mayday on Holderness', for example, or of the mortal struggle hidden beneath 'To Paint a Water-lily'. Thrushes, for Hughes, are ''Nothing but bounce and stab/And a ravening second''. Where Hughes is fascinated by the intricacies of violence in the compost-heap or attracted by pike, ''Killers from the egg'', who nevertheless

> move, stunned by their own grandeur,
> Over a bed of emerald, silhouette
> Of submarine delicacy and horror,
> A hundred feet long in their world

Heaney very deliberately turns away. His title-poem, 'Death of a Naturalist', tells us as much. Where Hughes watches his master-pike behind glass swallow all his fellows and accepts, when fishing, pike ''so immense and old'' that they are as legendary as the depths that hold them, the boy Heaney, having filled his jampots happily enough with the ''jellied/Specks'' of frogspawn, is ultimately ap-palled by the army of frogs on the flaxdam:

> Right down the dam gross-bellied frogs were cocked
> On sods; their loose necks pulsed like sails. Some hopped:
> The slap and hop were obscene threats. Some sat
> Poised like mud grenades, their blunt heads farting.
> I sickened, turned and ran. The great slime kings
> Were gathered there for vengeance and I knew
> That if I dipped my hand the spawn would clutch it.

There is no acceptance here, no marvelling at an intricate and dangerous Nature for its own sake. On the contrary, the centre of Heaney's poetry is always human: the emphasis is on the boy's imagination, on the shaping of the natural world by increasing skill and understanding, in the end on the naturalness of man's centrality in his chosen environment. The two or three poems of fear are not based on the innate hostility of Nature: the imaginings are those of a child and ultimately erroneous. In 'The Barn', a particularly successful poem in this genre, inanimate objects—two-lugged sacks of corn, cobwebs that suggest bats, a "mouse-grey" concrete floor—work on the natural timidity of the child. Half-seen fixtures, bright eyes in corners, cobwebs clogging the lungs, are all potent in creating terror:

> The dark gulfed like a roof-space. I was chaff
> To be pecked up when birds shot through the air-slits.
> I lay face-down to shun the fear above.
> The two-lugged sacks moved in like great blind rats.

The hostility is not real, as with Hughes's thrushes, "More coiled steel than living": it is the frightened boy who puts lugs on the sacks. Moreover, Heaney has no interest in a Nature whose systems, checks and balances, whose onsets of death and means of survival continue independently of Man. He is not concerned with the elucidation of any kind of biological order. The poet himself, and beyond him his family, his family's tradition in one particular place, and the terms on which that tradition has been hacked out, so to speak, from the natural environment—these are at the centre of Heaney's poetic intention. The poems of fear are no more than an expression of inexperience, of apprenticeship in that tradition. Some of them point to a state of mind that others, like 'An Advancement of Learning', show the power to depart from.

What Heaney owes to Hughes, then, is a subject-matter that is rural, ungenteel and treated with force, not any kind of interpretation of that subject-matter. Indeed, where Heaney appears to come

closest to Hughes, as in 'The Early Purges' and 'Cow in Calf' there
is a half-heartedness about his conclusion which of itself places a distance between them. For where Hughes is all idea—and it is in idea,
in concept that the force really lies, with language some way
after—Heaney is ultimately all language. By this I mean not empty
rhetoric but a language which carries in itself the tough, the feel, the
apprehension of a solid world which, if in no sense polite or academic, is a world in which the poet has slowly made his way, deeply
conscious of its emanations (which are part of his inheritance) but
also aware that his own powers and interests are taking him out of it.
Ted Hughes in *Lupercal* is coming into the inheritance of his in-
credible, non-human world: Heaney has come out of his hard but
essentially human one and turns back to recreate it before it begins
to fade slowly from the forefront of living.

It is time now to look closely at the particular qualities of language
that Seamus Heaney brings to the recall of the tradition from which
he has moved away. Gerard Manley Hopkins, he tells us, was the
poet who influenced his early style. His "ear", he says, "was
educated" by Hopkins[3]. In retrospect he believes that the peculiar
regional characteristics of the Northern Ireland voice—perhaps,
even more specifically, the County Derry voice—produced in him a
natural affinity for "the heavily accented consonantal noise" of
Hopkins[4]. That is perhaps the more true because, while it may be
the tautness of Hopkins's line and the inventiveness of his vocabu-
lary that most quickly strikes another reader, it is certainly the battery of consonants that attracts Heaney.

The opening poem, 'Digging'—"a big coarse-grained navvy of a
poem", as its author calls it[5]—was written in the summer of 1964[6].
It was the first instance, Heaney believes, of his "finding a voice"[7],
the first poem in which his "*feel* had got into words"[8]. It also
presents him as overtly determining his approach to the relation of
past and present ways of life.

> Between my finger and my thumb
> The squat pen rests; snug as a gun.

The consonantal mis-rhyme here perhaps suggests the gap between
the hand, the symbol of family inheritance, and the newly acquired
weapon. Whether that be so or no, the consonantal *g*s (with some
help from *mb* and a number of onrunning *n*s) proclaim what the
words *squat* and *gun* first announced, that an alien force is being
applied to this older world and that there will be some squaring

down and shaping too (beyond what the casual eye discerns). The
concluding lines of the poem reiterate and strengthen this intention.

> Between my finger and my thumb
> The squat pen rests.

> I'll dig with it.

This determination to force and reshape the remembered world is
the more noticeable because in the heart of the poem there is quite a
different feeling. The poet's father, the skilled digger, is at work. In
old age he may present "a straining rump" but the prime, original
memory is one of the rhythm of a precise technique:

> The coarse boot nestled on the lug, the shaft
> Against the inside knee was levered firmly . . .

That was in digging potatoes. Out on the peat moor there was an
equal rhythm.

> Nicking and slicing neatly, heaving sods
> Over his shoulder, going down and down
> For the good turf. Digging.

Phrases like "the squelch and slap/Of soggy peat" alliterate the
harsh intractability of the environment, but through that intractability skill makes its way: it is "the curt cuts of an edge/Through
living roots" that echo in the son's mind. There is victory there, but
not one that the poet can repeat. He has no such skill. Perhaps that
is why, with the technique of words that he has acquired, he chooses
to emphasise force rather than skill, to pick up a pen that is "squat"
and to bludgeon out the shape of a durable and solid world. It is a
world conveyed much less in essence or idea than in the sound and
feel of its objective parts. Perhaps that is why 'Digging' has stanzas
but no regularity of line or structure. It is not so much felt *in toto* as
hammered together.

   In the knocking-together of this world the texture of the writing is
crucial. A battery of consonants is employed to communicate sound
and solidity. 'Churning Day', which begins with "four crocks . . .
large pottery bombs" in the small pantry (again the imagery of
force) continues like this:

> After the hot brewery of gland, cud and udder
> cool porous earthenware fermented the buttermilk
> for churning day, when the hooped churn was scoured
> with plumping kettles and the busy scrubber
> echoed daintily on the seasoned wood.
> It stood then, purified, on the flagged kitchen floor.

Groups of consonants signal the various stages in the process. The *b*s, *g*s and *d*s of the first line are succeeded by the *c*s, *p*s, *b*s and *f*s of a cooler state: these are soon pushed out by words like *scoured*, *plumping* and *scrubber* and, despite a quieter interlude marked by the word *daintily*, the final impression is of the stilled buttermilk, signified by the consonant *p*, contrasted with *flagged kitchen floor*, the sound-symbol of incessant busyness and the hard to-fro of many feet. When peace returns and churning day is over, Heaney knows instinctively how to echo in miniature, in the minds of the participants, the sound and feel of that day: there remain

> the pat and slap of small spades on wet lumps

Both sound and action scaled down.

This attention to texture, visible again in poems like 'Blackberry-Picking' and 'The Barn', is not merely unusual: it is a very considerable achievement. But it is an achievement that almost necessarily squeezes out other important elements in good writing. Despite the regular stanzas of 'The Barn', for example, structure gets less than its share of attention. Indeed, it is not until the consonantal hammering is modified and becomes more occasional that one can better tell whether Seamus Heaney has an ear for a finely crafted line. So long as the pen is "squat" and gunlike it has to be a deeply felt rhythm (like that of his father's digging) that is not overwhelmed by sheer noise and weight. As the book proceeds, however, the heaviness and cumbersomeness of the rural scene are less emphasised: the style that is deliberately attached to physical objects and the slow processes of the country begins to give way to another kind of durability, that of history and family tradition. The poem 'Follower' is transitional in this respect. While the picture of the poet's father ploughing is put together in the sharp, metallic-sounding manner that the chink and click of the process suggest to the ear, the control implicit in this weakens as the poet depicts his own failure ever to achieve the rhythm intrinsic to this "mistery". At the end of the

poem it is the father-son relationship, reversed, that holds the com-
position together, and the echoes are no longer the echoes of a set
and understood rhythm but of "stumbling". Before the change
began, "my father", the poet says

> would set the wing
> And fit the bright steel-pointed sock.
> The sod rolled over without breaking.
> At the headrig, with a single pluck
>
> Of reins, the sweating team turned round
> And back into the land.

These lines are sharp with *k*s, interspaced with duller-sounding *d*s
and *g*s to give the feel of the heaviness of the land and, in line five,
some intrusive *n*s to simulate the team's freer running momentarily
at the headland (or "headrig"). Then, the son, the little boy, the follower, "was a nuisance, tripping, falling,/Yapping always". There
is no control here, no rhythm.

> But today
> It is my father who keeps stumbling
> Behind me, and will not go away.

This is a totally successful and moving image that transforms the
poem and sets the original control and expertise in its limited, past
and essentially emotional place. Texture has been used effectively
for contrast in the earlier poems, as we have seen, but the use of a
concluding image to "top up" the incipient emotion in 'Follower'
subordinates the textural changes to the overall intention of the
poem in a new and effective manner.

'Ancestral Photograph', one of the most successful poems in the
book, demonstrates further how bucolic heaviness can be quickened
and enlivened by a more effective personal and emotional element.
It opens with a portrait of the poet's great-uncle:

> Jaws puff round and solid as a turnip,
> Dead eyes are statues and the upper lip
> Bullies the heavy mouth down to a droop.
> A bowler suggests the stage Irishman
> Whole look has two parts scorn, two parts dead pan.
> His silver watch chain girds him like a hoop.

In the first three lines of this stanza the dominating *p*s, *d*s and *b*s
create the impression of a rather forbidding solidity, but in the next

three the *n*s flatten it into the photograph again and the *hoop* of the last line is just enough, with its reminder *p*, to *gird* (as one line itself declares) the two parts of the impression together. The second stanza has more *n*s, is fainter because the photo is no longer in place on the wall, and when the remainder of the poem settles to a recollection of uncle and nephew (the poet's father) smacking hands over a bargain at fair-days, the language has a forthright rough-and-readiness but no consistent consonantal hammering. Indeed, in this poem, as in 'Follower', the stanzas are regular: the rhyme-scheme *aabccb* is equally so, except in stanza three where *aab* is followed by *ccc*, justifiable perhaps because it is in these lines that the fair-day bargain is struck (the repeating rhyme suggesting unity). One becomes aware, too, of the kinds of rhymes which, though in no sense outrageous, are sufficiently unusual to obviate the smallest feeling of rhythmic dullness and predictability. *Cattle/Wall*, *then/bargain*, *still/chronicle*, *stick/attic*—these help to maintain wayward, stumbling movement in the poem, a movement entirely in keeping with cautious farmers and hesitant cattle.

A more flexible, less emphatic style appears more and more as the book proceeds. But it must not be too readily inferred that success necessarily follows this development. Where the sheer thickness of texture held up poems like 'Blackberry-Picking' and 'Churning Day' whether or not there was a conclusion that could be felt neatly to end the theme, poems where words count less for their own sake and more for the development of the idea need to be more certain of their ultimate point. 'The Early Purges', for example (though this has a thicker texture than some) falls to an unimaginative, even prosy, ending, and 'Honeymoon Flight', too, does not know how to conclude. 'Dawn Shoot', again, is *so* rough and ready, the language *so* subordinated to the structure of the narrative, that it barely avoids, in parts, the rhythms natural to prose. It becomes plain, in fact, that the later poems of the book are as uneven as one might expect of apprentice work (observation of which inclines me, on no deeper examination, to the belief that many of them are *earlier* than the return-to-childhood poems with which the book opens). But here and there are pieces where the conclusion is as deft and satisfying as idea and verbal organisation have been throughout, poems like 'Synge on Aran', 'Saint Francis and the Birds' and 'Trout'. Even 'Docker', which falls away a little, opens superbly, despite the annoying ploy of making the title work within the poem:

> There, in the corner, staring at his drink.
> The cap juts like a gantry's crossbeam,
> Cowling plated forehead and sledgehead jaw.
> Speech is clamped in the lips' vice.

But the impression given by these later poems collectively is of a desultoriness, of a lack of cohesion. There are only two indications of a future direction. The first lies in the two historical poems, 'For the Commander of the Eliza', well turned and neatly ironic, and 'At a Potato Digging', where a recall of the famine of 'forty-five' is stitched a little uneasily (as one section) into the sharp visual description of the present which constitute almost three-quarters of the whole. Both these pieces arise naturally from the heritage of the poor on the land: they carry with them an ineradicable memory of what it is to be hungry, starving even, when the meagre harvest fails. They point a way forward, when the scenes of childhood no longer occupy the forefront, to the poet's more developed sympathies. The second indication of direction, however, is perhaps the more important in the short term—that is, within the context of *Death of a Naturalist*. There are four poems here which sketch in the poet's more mature autobiography, two in terms of emotional and psychological development, two in the more pregnant ambience of the poetry which may come to be written. 'An Advancement of Learning', one of the most mature and finished poems in the book, shows the poet overcoming his fear of a rat, and 'Twice Shy' embodies a very uncertain victory over nerves in dealing with a woman. The association of *rat* and *woman* in the last sentence sounds excessively uncomplimentary to the latter, but this essay is not an exercise in male chauvinism of the bitterest kind. Seamus Heaney does link the two poems, well separated as they are in the book, with a single symbol. In 'An Advancement of Learning' the poet takes the embankment path: he establishes "a bridgehead" when he turns to outstare the rat and his crossing the bridge is the mark of ultimate victory over his fears. In 'Twice Shy' (a title whose ambiguity makes it of less use than it might be) the two potential lovers cross the river to take the embankment walk (no doubt a firm declaration of intent on the part of both) but fail, out of tenseness and uncertainty, to consolidate that declaration. In the end the crossing is not what is important, because the would-be lovers have more in common with the river—

> Still waters running deep
> Along the embankment walk.

Their final state, indeed, is not *across* the bridge at all. Noticeable, in passing, are the short lines of this poem: full of movement as they are, they are held tight (and taut) in closely-rhyming six-line stanzas. The nervousness of the two participants is admirably conveyed in the structure of the poem: once again meaning comes as much out of sound and feel as what is overtly said.

Of the two poems that are intended to map the path the poet (rather than the man) has followed, one, 'Poem (for Marie)' has been briefly discussed already. From within the fold of the love he has found as an adult he intends to *perfect* "the child/Whose small imperfect limits would keep breaking". In other words, he will look back and settle that small world with his own poetic order (as he does in the early poems of the book) before attempting to order the world of his maturity. The other poem, 'Personal Helicon', seeks to *link* his childhood experience, compelling but "scaresome" too, with the adult experience of writing poetry. The image Heaney uses is that of Narcissus outgrown.

> As a child, they could not keep me from wells
> And old pumps with buckets and windlasses.
> I loved the dark drop, the trapped sky, the smells
> Of water weed, fungus and dank moss.

One well afforded a "rich crash" when the bucket hit the bottom but had no reflection: in another he could see a white face hovering on the water, but only after dragging out "long roots from the soft mulch":

> Others had echoes, gave back your own call
> With a clean new music in it.

All these wells were the scene of juvenile attempts, under a particular compulsion, at self-discovery—the long roots at the bottom and the sound of the voice with the clean *new* music in it.

> Now, to pry into roots, to finger slime,
> To stare big-eyed Narcissus, into some spring
> Is beneath all adult dignity. I rhyme
> To see myself, to set the darkness echoing.

This is an opaque but exhilarating conclusion. The poet does not know where he is going or what he will find, but the writing of poetry is itself a kind of compass: it is by examining himself, as he does in writing, that he begins to know direction. And the "sky" is no longer "trapped". Childish, limited explorations, perhaps Narcissistic in ultimate explanation, will no longer serve: "To see myself" is not to admire but to learn, to discover that 'I' who has to shape the darkness round about.

'Personal Helicon', its accomplishment apart, unites the poems of childhood with those of a greater maturity in an expanded image which is both subtle and poignant. It also concludes the book in another sense. The self-examination it suggests has produced little of direction as yet. Poetry has been discovered as an instrument: it has the power to move its creator fast and far but has so far engaged no more than a low gear in its departure from that first "trapped sky". And that is an apt comment on *Death of a Naturalist* as a collection. Its technical quality is already high: as against occasional miscalculations, such as 'Poor Women in a City Church', where two-syllabled, moving, balancing words are supposed to "still" the "Old dough-faced women with black shawls" one can point to passages of great virtuosity, like the description of the rat in 'An Advancement of Learning':

> He clockworked aimlessly a while,
> Stopped, back hunched and glistening,
> Ears plastered down on his knobbed skull. . . .

The feeling for different kinds of language is already well developed: texture and structure are seen as aids to meaning. But as Heaney's comparative youth would suggest, the poems that represent his early manhood, however well formed, do not cohere sufficiently to draw the poet's 'character' and the volume makes its mark on the reader far more because of the decision to go back and hammer out the relative simplicities of childhood in a language which, whatever criticism may be made of it, is unmistakably loud and confident. The Seamus Heaney of *North* is barely hinted at and 'divided Ireland', as a theme which must necessarily thrust itself into the poet's consciousness, is still, in 1966, in the future. But the talent, and the force with which it is used in the poems of childhood, gave immediate notice to the literary world: Northern Ireland had a new and promising young poet.

NOTES

1. Alvarez, A. ed. *The New Poetry*, London 1962. p. 21.
2. *Preoccupations*, p. 19.
3. *Ploughshares*, Vol. 5, No. 3 (1979), p. 13.
4. *Preoccupations*, p. 44.
5. *Ibid*, p. 43.
6. *Ibid*, p. 41.
7. *Ibid*, p. 43.
8. *Ibid*, p. 41.

DICK DAVIS

Door into the Dark

Door into the Dark

"Fear is the emotion that the muse thrives on. That's always there". Seamus Heaney in conversation with John Haffenden.

The child in *Death of a Naturalist* is educated by moments of sickening fear; "I sickened, turned, and ran" (the title poem), "My throat sickened so quickly that/I turned down the path in cold sweat" ('An Advancement of Learning'), "the fear came back/When Dan . . ./ . . . with a sickening tug, pulled old hen's necks" ('The Early Purges'). Nausea, fear and insight are intimately tangled: an unsuspected darkness opens before the child and threatens to engulf him ("I knew/That if I dipped my hand the spawn would clutch it"). In these poems the darkness is associated with an uncontrollable fecundity, a pullulation of alien, secret, absorbing life—rats, frog-spawn, even the familiar cat suddenly produces a litter of kittens that makes its unnerving demands of responsibility and murder on the child. The speaker of the poems in Heaney's first two books is like the father in his poem 'Follower', "His eye/Narrowed and angled at the ground,/Mapping the furrow exactly"—his vision is held largely at ground level, tracing the contours of earth and the ways in which it will open before the feet to give on to pond, lough, well, clay-pit, bog, shore-line. In each case solidity gives way to what is viscid, liquid, ungraspable, untrustworthy.

Two remarks from Heaney's interview with John Haffenden seem relevant. One is concerned with a distinction between what he calls the "Antaeus" sensibility and the "Hercules" sensibility. Hercules and Antaeus wrestle; Antaeus is the son of Gē, the Earth-mother, and whenever he is thrown he gains renewed strength from his contact with the earth. Hercules can only overcome him by lifting him away from the earth, into the air. If the latter, "the possibility of the play of intelligence", becomes a shaping factor in his later books. *Death of a Naturalist* and *Door into the Dark* are both moulded by the poet as Antaeus—"a native, an earth-grubber, in touch with the ground". But this suggests that the poet is at home with the ground in which he grubs and from which he draws his strength; it does not account for the fascinated nausea, that sense of being hypnotised by the alien and bestial (like the child in Richard Wilbur's 'Beasts' who feels himself sucked downwards by "the degradation/Of the heavy streams") which haunts the early poems. The other remark concerns his Catholic upbringing; "The reality that was addressed was maternal, and the posture was one of supplication". If the reality here indicated is supernatural the description applies equally to the gross material reality of his poetry—which is a fecund, breeding darkness at which the child stares in supplicatory horror.

One who is intimate with this principle risks that absorption the frog-spawn threatened; "Bridegroom to the goddess,/She tightened her torc on him/And opened her fen". The earth presents itself as both mother and lover; the sexual implication of "and opened her fen" is unmistakable, as is that of the closing line of 'Bogland', *Door into the Dark*'s last poem, "The wet centre is bottomless" (the reader is reminded of Lawrence's fig and its "moist conductivity towards the centre", though Heaney's verse never has the overbearing male aggression which femininity seems to awaken in Lawrence). If the natural world is seen as feminine in Heaney's poetry—a fecund, pullulating maternal principle, an all-absorbing, threatening lover— the male poet's attitude towards this world is well described as "one of supplication", a mingled need and fear, erotic in its intensity and at times almost necrophiliac in its bewitched obsession.

The impulse of the child in *Death of a Naturalist* when confronted with such, to him obscene, fecundity is to run ("I sickened, turned, and ran") and the poems that deal with such encounters can be seen as on one level acts of private exorcism; but the adult's—the poet's—reaction is firstly to outstare the darkness (the transition is recorded in 'An Advancement of Learning' as the crossing of a rather neatly symbolic bridge, "I stared him out/Forgetting how I used to panic/. . . I stared a minute after him./Then I walked on and crossed the bridge") and then to attempt to come to terms with it, to explore it, to—to use an archaic word Heaney employs more than once—"tent" it. This exploration, this peering down wells, digging, fishing, exhumation, rescuing from oblivion, probing of secrecy and inwardness, concern with the subaqueous and subterranean which is so typical of the poems in Heaney's first three books, is not carried out in a spirit of explication and explanation but of a communion with mystery. Again the archetype of Marian devotion seems apposite—his tentings of the obscure are less an attempt to bring to light than to allow the author to enter the feared, maternal darkness— or at the least receive some confirming intimation of its potency. The very title of his second book, *Door into the Dark*, suggests a determination to find a way into that darkness, to conquer the child's terror by communion with its source.

The first poem of the book, 'Night-Piece', takes us into the darkness with the child's reluctance still clinging to the words, it begins as a return to nightmare or shame—"Must you know it again"— and the hint of nightmare and nausea lingers in other poems which suggest a fear of inward, psychological darkness, a fear of going too deeply into the self as much as a fear of external threat—"The next stroke/Found a man's head under the hook". But though the ground beneath the feet is still characterised as a glutinous, absorbing matrix, the poet is more even-toned in his exploration, more in control of his circling fascination; this is apparent if we compare the end of 'Death of a Naturalist'—"The great slime kings/Were gathered there for vengeance and I knew/That if I dipped my hand the spawn would clutch it"—with the end of 'Bann Clay' from *Door into the Dark*;

> Under the humus and roots
> This smooth weight. I labour
> Towards it still. It holds and gluts.

The poet's connection with his subject is willed—"I labour towards it"—rather than forced upon him as an unwelcome revelation, and the language records not only the immediacy of a single experience but a whole attitude of mind, so that digging for the clay that "holds and gluts" becomes a metaphor of wider and more general exhumations, a deliberate search for a "door into the dark". The darkness that the clay is and implies is the darkness of the unfathomable past, "Above it, the webbed marsh is new,/Even the clutch of Mesolithic/ Flints" and the door into the dark which Heaney seeks is not only a way into the ahistorical mystery of birth and fecundity, of the landscape's feared maternal presence, but into the obscurity of its past. The past is buried but persistent in the land and this paradoxical presence of what is gone is the subject of 'Relic of Memory", an evocation of wood petrified by the waters of a lough, of past life held as if by an act of the landscape's memory. This is a darkness the poet can explore without that frisson of fear which haunts his poems on the

darkness of the natural world—it seems an altogether more scholarly, antiquarian foray into night, prompted as much by *pietas* as
terror. The last poem of *Door into the Dark*, 'Bogland', looks forward
to the ways in which Heaney later used the preserving waters of the
bog as an image of "the memory of the landscape, or as a landscape
that remembered everything that had happened in and to it"; in the
poems on the Bog people, prompted by Glob's book, this sense of
pietas and wonder mingles with the maternal/erotic fear that ghosts
Heaney's apprehension of the natural world.

The evocation of the subterranean and subaqueous in Heaney's
poetry is then in part an exploration of that alarming potency of the
natural world revealed to him as a child—a potency both destructive
and fecund (in 'A Lough Neagh Sequence' we begin with simple de-
struction, "The lough will claim a victim every year" and end with
a typical image of life as an obscene, devouring force: "The lice,
they said, would gang up/Into a mealy rope/And drag him, small,
dirty, doomed//Down to the water".) and it is also an attempt to
enter into the quiddity of the past, to record and evoke "the memory
of the landscape". But it is impossible to read these poems on the
poet's wary, inquiring, fascinated probings of darkness without also
being aware of them as presenting paradigms for the nature of the
poems themselves. Heaney is no aesthete, and the inward source of
his work is clearly something far more pre-literate, pre-intellectual,
in his make-up than the production of artefacts. Nevertheless the
"door into the dark" of the title has undeniable implications of a
door into that uncharted darkness of the subconscious from which
the material of poetry surfaces with the silent importuning insistence
of Glob's Tollund Man exhumed from his bog. As with the image of
the bog itself, Heaney develops the notion of a poem as the discovery
of what is buried. In his books subsequent to *Door into the Dark*—
particularly in *Wintering Out* and in *North*—the language itself is seen
as a repository parallel to that of the poet's consciousness, preserving, petrifying, shaping experience in its own dark medium.

Three poems in *Door into the Dark* are concerned with enclosed
dark spaces which house an intensity of concentrated life; there is
'The Forge', from which the book's title comes—the poet is outside
and can only dimly make out the violent, noisy labour within; there
is 'The Outlaw', concerned with a stud-bull kept in a dark shed
which the child of the poem cannot enter; and there is 'In Gallurus
Oratory'—here the poet is able to enter the darkness because the
community that packed it has gone. In each case the poet sees or

imagines this life emerging from the darkness into light as a sense of expansion and release—"The sea a censor and the grass a flame"— though bull and smith must re-enter their stifling cells. These man-made darknesses, oratory, byre, forge—though their violence and potency seem to exclude the poet—act as symbols of a desired inten-sity of labour and authenticity, as if the poet takes as heroic para-digms the bull's potency, the smith's strength and skill, the religious community's passion and commitment. And what are such potency, skill and commitment to be used by a poet for but to make poetry? To similar effect 'Rite of Spring', 'Undine' and 'Bann Clay' utilise images of blocked or clogged water-channels—pump, ditch, drain— to suggest a pent-up energy suddenly freed; again the descriptions of released vigour suggest parallels with the act of poetic creation, a freeing of impulse or inspiration, a welling up of language, so that Undine seems like Heaney's feminine Nature made benign, an inti-mate chortling muse.

Heaney's use of explorative forays into darkness (and the release from darkness) to suggest a poetic strategy implies that he sees the poet largely as a *trouvère*, a finder, rather than as the Greek maker. But 'The Forge', if we take it as being in some degree a poem about poetry, indicates that he is also concerned with the poet as crafts-man. The forge is a "cave of making", and as Auden wrote on that subject:

> For this and for all enclosures like it the archetype
> is Weland's stithy . . .

Similarly, 'Thatcher' can also be read as a submerged poem about poets—the poet's regard for the thatcher is a regard for a laconic, unfussy skill, for a "mystery" in the old sense, as is his regard for the smith of 'The Forge'; both carry with them the glamour of the maker which we feel the young poet anxious to emulate. If he will dig with his pen, in the words of *Death of a Naturalist*, he will also forge, twist, sharpen and stitch.

"Twist" "sharpen" and "stitch" are words taken from 'Thatcher' and there are many more such verbs in the piece—"poked", "flicked", "honed", "snipped", "Flushed"—all of them con-cerned with what is immediate, physical, tangible. One of the chief reasons for the tang of authenticity which so much of Heaney's poetry brings with it is the fitness of the language he uses for the vision he has to record. His subjects—the fecundity of the landscape, the packed density of darkness, (geological, mythical, historical) that

awaits the poet's exploration, the intimately visceral emotions of
fear, nausea and sudden wonder—are presented in almost wholly
physical language. It is a cliché of modern poetic theory that the language of poetry should not be abstract—a cliché that has closed off
vast areas of our experience to poets and led to the ignoring of poets
who have chosen to address such areas in appropriate language—
but it is a cliché which in Heaney's case has a local validity. His
early poetry seeks not to understand but to evoke, not to put into
perspective but to see in tranced close-up. It is visceral rather than
intellectual, making its effects by the exploration of image rather
than by discursive argument, precision of syntax or metrical dexterity; it seeks density rather than clarity. Things, not ideas, particularly living things and their textures (slimy, shaggy, scaly, creamy,
tacky, jellied, mealy, jaggy—all adjectives from *Door into the Dark*)
haunt Heaney's imagination in this book, and his language is relent-
lessly physical, packed, dense with what he has called "the redemp-
tive quality of the dialect, of the guttural, the illiterate self"; when
he says of the Bann Clay that "it holds and gluts" the function of the
word "glut" is as much onomatopaeic as semantic, it communicates
as much by sheer physical sound as by meaning. This is a poetry
which asks us to believe that truth is buried, dark, probably frightening, immanent rather than transcendent, and that when it is discovered it brings something of the smothering airless underground
with it.

Certainly this is not the only possible kind of poetry—and some
critics have written, foolishly enough, as if it were (as though the
words "concrete" and "disturbing" were an automatic Seal of
Good Poem Making)—but it is a kind of poetry clearly at one with
Heaney's temperament when he wrote *Door into the Dark*, and a kind
he writes with a maker's sure skill, the *trouvère's* instinct for a yielding
way into darkness.

PHILIP HOBSBAUM

Craft and Technique in *Wintering Out*

Craft and Technique in *Wintering Out*

Seamus Heaney is one of the most talented poets now writing; he is also one of the most uneven. There is nothing in his work that is inept, but he himself has differentiated craft from technique. "Craft is what you can learn from other verse. Craft is the skill of making. It wins competitions in the *Irish Times* or the *New Statesman*." Seamus Heaney has won all of the competitions, and deserves to; no poet has had more startling success in his youth. But technique, as Heaney so wisely says, "involves not only a poet's way with words . . . it involves also a definition of his stance towards life, a definition of his own reality". It is here we may feel that the poetry of Seamus Heaney acts only intermittently.

Seamus Heaney's craft of verse is astonishingly certain: so much so, that at times it seems to support itself, to go on speaking under the impetus of language. There is a kind of Heaneyspeak that borders self-parody. It is summed up by a poem, 'Nerthus':

> For beauty, say an ash-fork staked in peat,
> Its long grains gathering to the gouged split;
>
> A seasoned, unsleeved taker of the weather,
> Where kesh and loaning finger out to heather.

It is this sort of writing that associates itself with tractors hitched to buckrakes, hands scuffled over the bake-board, the dulse-brown shroud, the bleb of the icicle, badgers dunting under the laurels, and a burnished bay-tree hung with the reek of silage. This, however 'true' it is, smells not of silage but the lamp: the lamp of a bright boy from St Columb's School, who studied Hopkins, Hardy and Frost at the right time and turned them to notable account. It is the snap-crackle-and-pop of diction; the very cud of memory.

Undoubtedly, this is what the reviewers like. One of them mistook Michael Longley and David Hammond, the distinguished poet and the distinguished musician who are joint dedicatees of *Wintering Out*, for two members of the I.R.A. shot by Brits in Ulster. One can imagine a misreading that would reconstruct the whole book as a sort of cairn erected to their memory. But, when Heaney speaks for Ireland, he does so in a way other than that.

> Then sometimes when the rosary was dragging
> mournfully on in the kitchen
> we would hear his step round the gable
>
> though not until after the litany
> would the knock come to the door
> and the casual whistle strike up
>
> on the doorstep. 'A right-looking night,'
> he might say, 'I was dandering by
> and says I, I might as well call . . .'
>
> 'The Other Side'

Language here is medium and meaning: it does not stand apart, as in the more self-consciously pastoral poems, like a separate carapace. It is the contrast between a definition of the Catholic way of life—"the rosary was dragging on/mournfully"—and that of the Protestant—"we would hear his step round the gable". The Catholic way is defined with rueful irony: Heaney is by no means uncritical of his side of the house. But, in his quiet manner, he indicates that it is indigenous. The Protestant is like a stranger in the dark outside, embarrassed by the lovemaking and the weeping within. One can approach him only on the prosaic level of inquiries about the weather or the price of grass-seed. To that extent Heaney's vision is angled, and it would be extraordinary if it were not. Yet what insight into the relationship between two distinct cultures is shown here! Heaney is not an intellectual. An intellectual, in the accepted sense, would not be able to present in this eidetic mode a contrast that can lead to conflict—

> When he would stand like that
> on the other side, white-haired,
> swinging his blackthorn
>
> at the marsh weeds,
> he prophesied above our scraggy acres,
> then turned away . . .

This is more than a visual image of a Protestant as seen by a Catholic.

That "prophesied" has overtones of the literal Word of the less can-
onical sector of the Old Testament. That antithesis of "*white*-
haired" and "*black*thorn" has the tang of Calvinist judgment. If
there is an influence in this poem, it is not the indulgence in Hopkins
or Hughes that wins plaudits from the critics, glad to recognise once
more what they have recognised already. Rather it is an influence so
absorbed that, as Leavis said of Eliot reworking Laforgue, it
amounts to originality:

> He stands in the doorway of his house
> A ragged sculpture of the wind . . .

This is Heaney's true predecessor, Patrick Kavanagh, whose craft
occasionally wobbled a bit but whose technique, as Heaney himself
has said, was certain. There are poems by Patrick Kavanagh that
any tyro could put right; but he is also the author of 'The Great
Hunger', a living contradiction to the critical belief that you cannot
have a long poem in the twentieth century. Heaney's eidolon of the
Black Protestant has learned from Kavanagh's description of
Maguire, the Monaghan hill-farmer; however, to learn thus is to be
not an apprentice but a master. When Heaney writes in this mode,
the poem seems to come at the reader from inside his psyche.

Yet such quality is intermittent. This may be in part a question of
metre. All too often, Heaney adopts a rhetorical manner along with
a rhythm, and a persona along with a rhetorical manner. In particular, his frequent adoption of a set quatrain is a limiting factor. It
constrains into family resemblance attitudes which seek to push
away from each other in quite different directions.

> We have no prairies
> To slice a big sun at evening—
> Everywhere the eye concedes to
> Encroaching horizon . . .
>
> > 'Bogland'

> Some day I will go to Aarhus
> To see his peat-brown head,
> The mild pods of his eyelids,
> His pointed skin cap . . .
>
> > 'The Tollund Man'

> It's a long time since I saw
> The afterbirth strung on the hedge
> As if the wind smarted
> And streamed bloodshot tears . . .
>
> 'First Calf'

This may be an attempt after the loose quatrain of Patrick Kavanagh in 'The Great Hunger' and elsewhere; a means of avoiding the exoticism of buckrake and bakeboard. But, though the craft is sure enough, it doesn't work with quite the same certainty of technique. The form, as Heaney uses it, is too pre-set, too compartmentalised. The point can be made briskly enough if we essay another comparison with Kavanagh—

> A dog lying on a torn jacket under a heeled-up cart,
> A horse nosing along the posied headland, trailing
> A rusty plough. Three heads hanging between wide-apart
> Legs. October playing a symphony on a slack wire paling . . .

This is not a stanza but a quatrain. The verse can be concertinaed in, as at the start of the quatrain following, or it can be drawn right out, as happens in the third line here—

> Wife and mother in one.
> When she died
> The knuckle-bones were cutting the skin of her son's backside
> And he was sixty-five . . .

The loose quatrain frees Kavanagh: he can play more tunes on it than any but the greatest poets have ever managed in free verse. But in Seamus Heaney the loose quatrain all too often circumscribes itself into a four-line stanza, and the effect is that of a good poet on his best behaviour.

> What she remembers
> Is his glistening back
> In the bath, his small boots
> In the ring of boots at her feet . . .
>
> 'Mother of the Groom'

To my ear, this seems rather flat: the admixture of metrical conformity and dispersed pararhyme makes that last line fall with a thud. Surely there should have been an ictus of some kind to redeem the inclination, immanent in the poem, towards sentimentality?

> Once soap would ease off
> The wedding ring
> That's bedded forever now
> In her clapping hand.

It is not exotic; nevertheless, there is a literariness here which goes along with a sense of anticlimax: we miss a redeeming irony which would have anticipated deflation. This is craft; it is not technique.

One dares to discriminate in this fashion because Seamus Heaney solves the problem on the very next page; in the adjunctive poem, 'Summer Home'. Significantly, this is in a remarkable free verse.

> Was it wind off the dumps
> or something in heat
>
> dogging us, the summer gone sour,
> a fouled nest incubating somewhere?
>   'Summer Home'

Metrically, this will bear a good deal of attention. Free verse is a blanket term, but this particular form of it pits one line against another, sacrificing no properties of internal and occasional rhyme and pararhyme to do so—

> Bushing the door, my arms full
> of wild cherry and rhododendron,
> I hear her small lost weeping
> through the hall, that bells and hoarsens
> on my name, my name.
>
> O love, here is the blame.

It is not only a matter of metrical dexterity. Right through this remarkable poem the submerged aspect of the home is touched upon: the lavatorial odours, the tension of proximity that can suppurate into rancour—

> These frank and falling blooms
> soon taint to a sweet chrism . . .
>
> My children weep out the hot foreign night.
> We walk the floor, my foul mouth takes it out
> On you . . .

Flowers can taint, the mouth that kisses and eats is the repository also of foulness.

But the poem itself contains the remedy. Partly it is a matter of its characteristic mode of repetition—"Attend. Anoint the wound . . ."; "O we tented our wound all right . . ."; "as you bend in the shower . . ."; "dawn/Attends the pillow . . .". That "attend-tented-bend-attend" sequence acts at once as spine to the poem, and as consolation.

Another key sequence is the sense of liquid washing the stains away, so that tears seem purgation and a shower becomes healing. The small lost weeping of Section II modulates into the dripping dark of the cave in Section V, with its genital overtones. The tiny call of the tuning-fork resets the pitch and indicates that all may become harmonious again.

Having said this, I do not want to lessen the sense that this is a poem that contains agony. That it creates in its nervous verse an implied reconciliation does not alter the antagonism of the attitudes that are to be reconciled. In a genuinely creative way, this has been learned from Robert Lowell. Like Lowell, it is set apart from the confessional poets by the dramatic feel given to a situation which, taken autobiographically, would be too painfully intimate to be read as literature.

The words to invoke are 'stylisation' and 'distance'. Only a fine technique—not a learned skill but a definition of stance—could justify the publication of experience such as this. One would say the same of *Life Studies*. What we are looking at in 'Summer Home' is a node of tension in a vulnerable marriage; but it is a marriage within a dramatic fiction. We are given an exquisite sense of the agony felt in assailing a loved one. It is a pain that is within the psyche. In this poem, as in the very different 'The Other Side', Seamus Heaney comes at us from within.

This is the work of Heaney that seems to me destined to last: a kind of psychic exploration in which form is so deployed as to become meaning. The writing of 'The Other Side' and of 'Summer Home' seems to have little in common; yet both poems are quite distinct from the "kesh and loaning" aspect of Heaney; distinct, too, from the repetitious siting of Tollund Man and Bog Queen; not in alluvial mud, but in tamed stanzas. What these poems I have singled out as distinctive have in common relates to such other poems as 'Honeymoon Flight', 'The Peninsula', 'Act of Union'; and, indeed, to one or two other poems not yet in the public domain, that may impress Seamus Heaney's regular audience pleasantly or otherwise as the case may be.

What I have suggested is that this poet, always good by current critical standards, has moments which transcend his established norm. One sign of his potential is the heuristic quality of his critical writing: such an essay as 'Feeling into Words' is likely to be pondered when nearly all structuralist discourse is dead. But, by the standard of this essay as well as that of his best published poems, the accolade must not fall on the shoulders of Seamus Heaney too soon or too heavily. It was not the author of the present article who made the distinction between craft and technique, although he has gladly adopted it as a means of discriminating and differentiating among Heaney's various works. Seamus Heaney has it in him to rival Robert Frost or Thomas Hardy, though he is unlikely to do so by taking any more from those particular poets than he has acquired already. What the critics of our day acclaim as achievement, those of the future may very well look back upon as promise.

ANNE STEVENSON

Stations: Seamus Heaney and the Sacred Sense of the Sensitive Self

Stations:
Seamus Heaney and the Sacred
Sense of the Sensitive Self

As long ago as 1975, Frank Ormsby's *Ulster Publications* brought out
a sequence of twenty-one prose poems by Seamus Heaney called
Stations. In a short introduction Heaney described the genesis of
these pieces—a genesis which began in California in 1970/71 but
which "rapidly came to a head" in 1974, a month after the introduction of internment in Belfast. What began, then, as a series
of psycho-autobiographical sketches, "attempts to touch what
Wordsworth called 'spots of time', moments at the very edge of consciousness" was delayed by the appearance of Geoffrey Hill's
Mercian Hymns ("What I had regarded as stolen marches in a form
new to me had been headed off by a work of complete authority")
but partly, too, by the hesitations of Heaney's political conscience.
Returning to Belfast from America, Heaney discovered that his "in-
trospection was not confident enough to pursue its direction."

If "direction" here means pursuit of the psychological sources of
Heaney's poetry—the searching-out of private epiphanies lost in the
all but unconscious memories of childhood—then *Stations* is as clear
a declaration as we have of Heaney's dilemma as a post-Romantic,
post-Freudian poet confronted by an impersonal, probably in-
soluble, national crisis. Let's ignore Heaney's Irishness for the present and look instead at his Romanticism. I assume we can agree
without prejudice that Heaney (like Lowell, whom lately he begins
to resemble) could not and would not have written quite as he has,
had it not been for the example of Wordsworth (and only *after*
Wordsworth, Yeats, Joyce and Patrick Kavanagh). For in Wordsworth we have the first instance in Britain of a poet in retreat from a
corrupting society and a doubtful religion, digging in and fortifying
the bastions of his own psyche. The poet as hero appears Romantic-
ally, of course, in Goethe and in Byron; yet it is in Wordsworth that
his *retreat* is most in evidence, his withdrawal from the world into a
sacred area of personal sensitivity; opposing to the world not only

Nature (this was a practice older than Shakespeare, older than Virgil) but, *in* Nature, a subjective, unrational self.

It would be simple-minded, indeed silly, to claim—as some critics have claimed—that this sacred sense of the self which is Heaney's well-spring of imagination is mere self-indulgence. For who is to say with certainty that a single poet's experience is, in fact, singular? Whitman's *Song of Myself* extended that 'self' into a kind of broad-casting device for the promulgation of ecstatic love. Wordsworth's more particular 'self' found in childhood and Nature a solace for frustrated revolutionary idealism. So each, in different ways, spoke for his age, or for the questing, Romantic spirit of that age.

In Heaney's case, though he speaks for *his* age, we perceive a difference. Political and philosophical idealisms no longer have the hold over our imaginations that they did during the nineteenth century. Nor are our notions of what is possible in human society as confident or as exuberant as those of pre-Freudian, pre-Jungian, pre-Nazi, or even pre-Vietnam Romantics. We are all of us sufferers from failure, a failure not so much of religion in any formal sense, but of Romanticism itself and the freedom to love and suffer that Romanticism, explicitly or inexplicitly, promoted as a dominant faith. Heaney, with his Wordsworthian instincts and gifts, has come to fame within a framework of doubt which, as in the case of Robert Lowell, is easily converted into guilt. In pursuit of nourishment for art, poets like Heaney are confronted with public pressure (a pressure they possibly imagine to be stronger than it is) to *do* something about a public situation. As an Irish Catholic in Ulster, Heaney should have something to say (such, I imagine, has been his own feeling). And in *North*, of course, he did find something to say; but that something did not quite answer the abiding and gnawing question of what, also, to *do*.

Understanding Heaney had, and still has, in abundance, and yet he casts "the stones of silence":

> I who have stood dumb
> when your betraying sisters,
> cauled in tar,
> wept by the railings,
>
> who would connive
> in civilized outrage
> yet understand the exact
> and tribal, intimate revenge.

North appeared in the same year as *Stations*—1975; so it would seem that in the poems of this period (written in the first half of the 1970's) Heaney imaginatively came to an understanding of his position through an exploration of a particular history and society. As Nature was for Wordsworth, the Bog People were for Heaney. Through them and their sacrifices Heaney reconciled himself, however painfully, to privately understanding "the exact, tribal" nature of the IRA's revenge. At the end of *North*, that most revealing of poems, 'Exposure', shows us Heaney's self as anti-hero full of "responsible tristia", but for what?

> I am neither internee nor informer;
> An inner émigré, grown long-haired
> And thoughtful; a wood-kerne
>
> Escaped from the massacre,
> Taking protective colouring
> From bole and bark . . .

Responsible for himself, then. In the exquisite poems of *North* Heaney is retreating into an area of personal sensitivity, just as Wordsworth did. But instead of looking outward from his hole into

> Ye Presence of Nature in the sky
> And on the earth! Ye Visions of the hills!
> And Souls of lonely places!

Heaney is compelled instead to look inwards and backwards, into himself and backwards into history, into the human bog. No wonder he feels he has missed "The once-in-a-lifetime portent,/The comet's pulsing rose."

In coming to—or digging himself into—this position in *North*, Heaney made some of his best poems—poems that paradoxically speak publicly of his failure, and out of this failure, reach successfully to a huge, not necessarily Irish audience. What he shares with his readers is not the Irish question, nor is it his personal grief (although that is there). No. What he shares, or manifests, is precisely failure itself—that 'failure' which in our time has become a hall-mark of honesty, that 'confession' which, in the work of Sylvia Plath, John Berryman, Robert Lowell and Geoffrey Hill, has cleared the air of false ideals, "Visions", "Presences" and mysticism itself. And if the strengths of the mode of confession—of failure— are such as to appeal to many of us, especially Americans, why should

poets worry about what to do or say about particular political situa-
tions—such as now in Ireland? Why not go on confessing failure in
the face of human unredeemability . . . confessing it very beautifully, as Heaney and Hill do?

Stations, I think, provides us with a hint of an answer to this
question. For *Stations* is not a book of poems, as *North* is, but a
collection of highly-charged prose pieces which Heaney asks to do
the work of poems. And this, for all their skill in language, they do
not quite do.

In these twenty-one pieces of carefully but artificially chosen language, the larger Heaney of the poems, the confessor, the inheritor
of the Great Bog, the Romantic in despair before his destiny, dis-
appears. We are left, instead, with twenty-one (to mark a coming of
age?) self-conscious entries in a diary of personal memories. And
these cut us out by their very artistry. We are left wanting either
more autobiography or more art; or perhaps *less* art and more context, more 'reality'.

An autobiography is not quite art because it purports to be the
story of a life. People's lives usually fascinate us, but not as art does.
What a man did and thought or wrote, what a person judged funny
or sad, what characters moulded his/her character, what happened
when and why . . . this is the stuff of human and empathetic appetite. We can never get enough of it. But when we are permitted only
tiny, exquisite, pre-chosen fragments of memory, as if in a
peepshow, we experience frustration. Curiously, the more beautifully these pieces 'read', the more frustrated we feel.

> Green air trawled over his arms and legs, the pods and stalks wore
> a fuzz of light. He caught a rod in each hand and jerked the whole
> tangle into life. Little tendrils unsprung, new veins lit in the shift-
> ing leaves, a caul of shadows stretched and netted round his head
> again. He sat listening, grateful as the call encroached.
>
> 'Cauled'
>
> Primroses grew in a damp single bunch out of the bank, implod-
> ing pallors, star plasm, nebula of May. He stared himself into an
> absence.
>
> 'Hedge-school'
>
> Through red seas of July the Orange drummers led a chosen
> people through their dream . . . The air grew dark, cloud-barred,
> a butcher's apron. The night hushed like a white-mothed reach of
> water, miles down-stream from the battle, skeins of blood still
> lazing in the channel.
>
> 'July'

Why, somehow, is the delicacy, the accuracy of these perceptions transformed by their language into sentimentality? Because, I suspect, the writer is writing of childhood experience with an adult eye on his effect. The perception is ingenious but false. The original experiences would not have called forth such eloquence; the language is like paint on an egg.

The importance of *Stations*, then, is that it explodes a contemporary myth we have come too easily to take for granted: the myth of the sensitive self as saviour, the myth that the 'self' can be salvaged, by art, from failure. What is felicitous in the poems of *North* becomes suspect in the more artificial mode of *Stations*. Perhaps prose-poetry always exhibits this weakness. I think of Oscar Wilde's sentimental fairy tales, of part of *Portraits of the Artist*, when Joyce forgets, momentarily, his genius for the comedy of the tragic. The spectacle of someone feeling sorry for himself or exceptionally tender about his younger self is common; we all cry over our past and love our losses. Heaney is too much of an artist to do that, and yet *Stations* is rosy with held-back tears.

It would be interesting to know whether Heaney wrote 'Exposure' before or after *Stations*, for the last Station is called 'Incertus', and it seems to fertilize the ground from which 'Exposure' sprang. I quote 'Incertus' in its entirety.

> I went disguised in it, pronouncing it with a soft church-latin c, tagging it under my efforts like a damp fuse. Uncertain. A shy soul fretting and all that. Expert obeisance.
>
> Oh, yes, I crept before I walked. The old pseudonym lies there like a mouldering tegument.

If this means that Heaney has left 'Incertus' behind him, that he has found himself enough in the bog poems and 'Singing School' to be able to lose himself, then *Stations is* a station, a stage in the progress of poet towards mastery of all the material he calls experience. Still, there is enough evidence, even in *North* and *Field Work*, to suggest that 'Incertus' is Heaney's worst enemy. For a man of sensibility and tenderness, it is too easy to take the soft option of a loving concentration on himself. Heaney is among the best poets living today, but if he is going to last, the self-bog, in the end, won't preserve him. It is good to know that he is translating Dante. That looks like the way out.

THE MANUSCRIPT DRAFTS OF THE POEM

North

I think technique is different from craft. Craft is what you can learn from other verse. Craft is the skill of making . . .
Technique is what turns, in Yeat's phrase, "the bundle of accident and incoherence that sits down to breakfast" into "an idea, something intended, complete".

Seamus Heaney: 'Feeling into Words'

Preoccupations: Selected Prose 1968-1978.

North Atlantic

I returned ~~to that long~~ strand, curved
~~when~~ ~~a ten se~~ like a shod, hammered under light,
~~its~~ tanned and glistening curve
and found only the secular
powers of the Atlantic thundering.

I faced the unmagical
imitations of Iceland,
the pathetic colonies
of Greenland,

I ~~imag~~ imagined the annual
~~I could contemplated~~ the boredom
of riding to the althing
the fear and hatred
between thickwitted farmers,

~~thy least fall~~

and suddenly those beautiful
adventurers, those lying
in Orkney or Dublin
measured against their long

swords rusting, those in the solid
belly of stone ships,
those hacked and ~~glinting~~ glinting
in the gravel of thawed streams
                ocean-deafened
were ~~small shouting~~ voices
warning me off, cursing
the mysterium of water.
The longship's swimming tongue

instructed me
against epiphanies—
Geography and trade,
~~the~~ thick-witted couplings and revenges,

the ~~bastards~~ and the terror
of the althing, lies and women,
~~the~~ exhaustions glorified as peace,
poets ~~keeping~~
              incubating the spilled blood.

NORTH ATLANTIC

I returned to that long strand,
curved like a shod, hammered under light,
and found only the secular
powers of the Atlantic thundering.

I faced the unmagical
invitations of Iceland,
the pathetic colonies of
of Greenland

And suddenly those beautiful
adventurers, those lying
in Orkney and Dublin
measured against their long

swords' rusting, those in the solid
belly of icum stone ships,
those hacked and glinting
in the gravel of thawed streams

were ocean-deafened voices
warning me off, cursing
the mysterium of water.
The longship's swimming tongue

instructed me
against epiphanies -
geography and trade,
thick-witted couplings and revenges,

the hatreds and the terror
of the althing, lies and women,
exhaustions nominated peace,
poets incubating the spilled blood.

Northerners

NORTH ATLANTIC

I returned to that long strand,
~~curved like a shed,~~ ~~hammered under light,~~ the beaten shod of the bay
and found only the secular
powers of the Atlantic thundering.

towards
I faced/the unmagical
invitations of Iceland,
the pathetic colonies ~~of~~
of Greenland

And suddenly those ~~beautiful~~ *fabulous*
adventurers, those lying
in Orkney and Dublin
measured against their long

swords' rusting, those in the solid
belly of ~~iron~~ stone ships,
those hacked and glinting
in the gravel of thawed streams

were ocean-deafened voices
warning me off, cursing
the mysterium of water.
The longship's swimming tongue

instructed me
~~against epiphanies -~~ it said Thor's hammer swung
geography and trade,
thick-witted couplings and revenges,

the hatreds and ~~the terror~~ behind backs
of the althing, lies and women,
exhaustions nominated peace,
~~poets~~ incubating the spilled blood.

memory

NORTHERNERS

I returned to that long strand,
the hammered shod of the bay,
and found only the secular
powers of the Atlantic thundering.

I faced towards the unmagical
invitations of Iceland,
the pathetic colonies
of Greenland

and suddenly those fabulous
adventurers, those lying
in Orkney and Dublin
measured against the long

swords' rusting, those in the solid
belly of stone ships,
those hacked and glinting
in the gravel of thawed streams

were ocean-deafened voices
warning me off, cursing
the mysterium of water.
The longship's swimming tongue

instructed me against epiphanies -
it said Thor's hammer swung
to geography and trade,
thick-witted couplings and revenges,

the hatreds and behind-backs
of the althing, lies and women,
exhaustions nominated peace,
memory incubating the spilled blood.

It said: "Lie down
in the word-hoard, follow
the warm of your thought
into the mound.

(Compose in darkness
imagining the moral light)

until it is bursts its mines
as an elaborate prow.
Compose in darkness,
imaging the ~~moral~~ light   our long winters,

(as the weather breathes
(live in, remembering
(our long winters

~~waiting for~~

Compose in darkness.
Expect ~~look for~~ ~~the~~ aurora borealis
~~the~~ in the long winter
of your art, but ~~not~~ no
a ~~the~~ ~~moral electric light.~~
cascade of moral light.

Keep your eye clear
as the icicle's pupil,
~~your heart~~ ~~double~~ weathered
as ~~a turf-stack~~ an upland turf-stack."

Trust the feel
of whatever nubbled treasures

your hands have known"

NORTH

I returned to a long strnad,
the hammered shod of a bay,
and found only the secular
power of the Atlantic thundering.

I faced ~~towards~~ the unmagical
invitations of Iceland,
the pathetic colonies
of Greenland,

and suddenly/those fabulous
~~adventurers~~,/those lying
in Orkney and Dublin/
measured against /their long swords

raiders

rusting,/those in the solid
belly of stone ships,
those hacked and glinting
in the gravel of thawed streams

were ocean-deafened voices
warning ~~me dt~~, cursing *the necessary*
the mysterium of water. *mystique of violence.*
The longship's swimming tongue
declared
~~instructed me~~ against epiphanies –
it said Thor's hammer swung
to geography and trade,
thick-witted couplings and revenges,

the hatreds and behind-backs
of the althing, lies and women,
exhaustions nominated peace,
memory incubating the spilled blood.

It said:"Lie down
in ths word-hoard, follow
the worm of your thought
into the mound.

Compose in darkness.
Expect aurora borealis
in the long ~~winter~~ of your art
but no cascade of moral light.

Keep your eye clear
as the ~~icicle's pupil~~, *bleb of the icicle,*
trust the feel of whatever nubbed
treasure your hands have known."

NORTH

I returned to a long strand,
the hammered shod of a bay,
and found only the secular
powers/of the Atlantic thundering.

I faced the unmagical
invitations of Iceland,
the pathetic colonies
of Greenland, and suddenly

those fabulous raiders,
those lying in Orkney and Dublin
measured against
their long swords rusting,

Those in the solid
belly of stone ships,
those hacked and glinting
in the gravel of thawed streams

were ocean-deafened voices
warning me, ~~cursing the necessary~~   *lifted again*
~~mystique of violence.~~   *in violence and epiphany*
The long ship's swimming tongue

~~declared against epiphanies~~ –   *was* ~~thick with repetition~~
it said Thor's hammer swung   *buoyant with hindsight –*
to geography and trade,
thick-witted couplings and revenges,

the hatreds and behind-backs
of the althing, lies and women,
exhautstions nominated peace,
memory incubating the spilled blood.

It said,"Lie down   *think enter*
in the word-hoard, follow   ~~of the gutter~~ *and gleam*
the worm of your thought   *of your brain's coiled furrows.*
into the mound.

Compose in darkness.
Expect aurora borealis
in the long foray of your art
but no cascade of light.

Keep your eye clear
as the bleb of the icicle,
trust ~~the feel of~~ whatever nubbed *treasures*
~~treasure~~/your hands have known."

North

I returned to a long strand,
the hammered shod of a bay,
and found only the secular
powers of the Atlantic thundering.

I faced the unmagical
invitations of Iceland,
the pathetic colonies
of Greenland, and suddenly

those fabulous raiders,
those lying in Orkney and Dublin
measured against
their long swords rusting,

those in the solid
belly of stone ships,
those hacked and glinting
in the gravel of thawed streams

were ocean deafened voices
warning me, lifted again
in violence and epiphany.
The longship's swimming tongue

was buoyant with hindsight—
it said Thor's hammer swung
to geography and trade,
thick-witted couplings and revenges,

the hatreds and behindbacks
of the althing, lies and women,
exhaustions nominated peace,
memory incubating the spilled blood.

It said, 'Lie down
in the word-hoard, burrow
the coil and gleam
of your furrowed brain.

Compose in darkness.
Expect aurora borealis
in the long foray
but no cascade of light.

Keep your eye clear
as the bleb of the icicle,
trust the feel of what nubbed treasure
your hands have known.'

EDNA LONGLEY

North: "Inner Emigré" or "Artful Voyeur"?

North: "Inner Emigré" or "Artful Voyeur"?

Seamus Heaney himself sees *North* (1975) as a culmination: "I'm certain that up to *North*, that that was one book; in a way it grows together and goes together"[1]. While broadly agreeing that the collection indeed crowns Heaney's previous poetry—in terms of merit as well as development—British and Irish commentators have diverged in their emphases. Although Anthony Thwaite, for instance, praises both style and content:

> These new poems have all the sensuousness of Mr. Heaney's earlier work, but refined and cut back to the bone. They are solid, beautifully wrought, expansively resonant. They recognize tragedy and violence without despairingly allowing them to flog human utterance into fragments . . .[2]

he does not probe the content more particularly or more politically, but falls back on the blurb ("Seamus Heaney has found a myth which allows him to articulate a vision of Ireland" etc.). Five years later Blake Morrison was to note: "with the exception of Conor Cruise O'Brien in the *Listener*, hardly anyone seemed interested in what it was that Heaney had to 'say' about Northern Ireland"[3]. There is nothing new in divergent perceptions on either side of the Irish Sea. (Or, conversely, in Irish writers simultaneously transmitting different messages to different audiences.) Still, O'Brien's informed response established a native line of comment on *North*, including contributions by its author, that raises the most fundamental questions about the relationship between literature and politics. He begins: "I had the uncanny feeling, reading these poems, of listening to the thing itself, the actual substance of historical agony and dissolution, the tragedy of a people in a place: the Catholics of Northern Ireland"[4]. Being so locally tuned in, O'Brien can dismiss simplistic comparisons between Heaney and Yeats: "Yeats was free to try, and did splendidly try, or try on, different relations to the tragedy: Heaney's relation to a deeper tragedy is fixed and pre-ordained."[5]

Is Heaney then, like 'The Tollund Man', "Bridegroom to the goddess"? His reaction to the Man's photograph deserves the much-abused term "epiphany", with its full Joycean connotations: a revelation of personal and artistic destiny expressed in religious language. Glossing the poem, he figures as pilgrim-acolyte: "My sense of occasion and almost awe as I vowed to go to pray to the Tollund Man and assist at his enshrined head"[6]; or as initiate into an order:

> when I wrote that poem I had a sense of crossing a line really, that
> my whole being was involved in the sense of—the root sense—of
> religion, being bonded to something, being bound to do some-
> thing. I felt it a vow . . ."[7]

The three parts of the poem itself might be tabulated as evocation ("his peat-brown head,/The mild pods of his eye-lids"), invocation ("I could . . . pray/Him to make germinate//The scattered, ambushed/Flesh of labourers"), and vocation ("Something of his sad freedom . . . Should come to me"). If nothing else, 'The Tollund Man' certainly germinated *North*. Insofar as Heaney's own role in the poems parallels that of the bridegroom-victims, does he really attain "sad freedom", or in fact sacrifice some imaginative liberty to that "dark-bowered queen", Kathleen ni Houlihan? Has tribal pre-ordination, or ordination, any petrifying effect on poetic life?

Interviewed (1977) by Seamus Deane about the relationship of the Ulster poets "to the Northern crisis", Heaney first volunteers the wise minimum: "The root of the troubles may have something in common with the root of the poetry"; then adduces some revealing autobiography:

> the very first poems I wrote, 'Docker' and one about Carrick-
> fergus Castle for instance, reveal this common root. The latter
> had William of Orange, English tourists and myself in it. A very
> inept sort of poem but my first attempts to speak, to make verse,
> faced the Northern sectarian problem. Then this went under-
> ground and I became very influenced by Hughes and one part of
> my temperament took over: the private county Derry childhood
> part of myself rather than the slightly aggravated young Catholic
> male part.[8]

The "slightly aggravated young Catholic male" did, however, occasionally surface before *Wintering Out* and his complete emergence from hibernation in *North*. As well as 'Docker' ("That fist would drop a hammer on a Catholic"), *Death of a Naturalist* contains two poems, 'At a Potato Digging' and 'For the Commander of the "Eliza" ', written in response to Cecil Woodham-Smith's *The Great Hunger*. The Commander, obliged by orders to withhold food from starving men in a rowing-boat, is haunted by an image that anticipates the boneyard of *North*: "Next day, like six bad smells, those living skulls/Drifted through the dark of bunks and hatches". In 'At a Potato Digging' a rather awkward metamorphosis changes potatoes as "live skulls, blind-eyed" into the real thing:

> Live skulls, blind-eyed, balanced on
> wild higgledy skeletons
> scoured the land in 'forty-five,
> wolfed the blighted root and died.

This transition is the hinge on which the poem turns from present to past (a better-oiled process in *North*). 'At a Potato Digging' starts out like an echo of Patrick Kavanagh's *The Great Hunger*: "Clay is the word and clay is the flesh/Where the potato-gatherers like mechanised scarecrows move/Along the side-fall of the hill" (Kavanagh); "A mechanical digger wrecks the drill,/Spins up a dark shower of roots and mould./Labourers swarm in behind . . ." (Heaney). But Kavanagh's title symbolises the starvation of the spirit in twentieth-century rural Ireland; his perspective on servitude to the land is local in place and time, whatever historic deprivations lurk in the background. As Heaney says, "The 'matter of Ireland', mythic, historical or literary forms no significant part of [Kavanagh's] material."[9] And again "At the bottom of Kavanagh's imagination there is no pagan queen, no mystique of the national, the mythic or the tribal."[10] (Does this make Kavanagh paradoxically more forward-looking than Heaney—a function of the North-South time-lag?). Heaney's potato-diggers undoubtedly guide him towards "the matter of Ireland", and towards his first embryonic fusion of Catholic experience in the North with the longer national history: "A people hungering from birth"; "and where potato diggers are/you still smell the running sore" (something rotten in the state of Ulster?). In another portent of the procedures of *North*, Heaney resolves the poem by drawing on a mixture of Christian and pagan ritual. The diggers who make "a seasonal altar of the sod", finally propitiate "the famine god" by spilling "Libations of cold tea".

'Requiem for the Croppies', the historical poem in *Door into the Dark*, joins the centuries more seamlessly and achieves a more organic, indeed germinal, resolution: "And in August the barley grew up out of the grave".

> [It] was written in 1966 when most poets in Ireland were straining to celebrate the anniversary of the 1916 Rising. That rising was the harvest of seeds sown in 1798, when revolutionary republican ideals and national feeling coalesced in the doctrines of Irish republicanism and in the rebellion of 1798—itself unsuccessful and savagely put down. The poem was born of and ended with an image of resurrection based on the fact that some time after the rebels were buried in common graves, these graves began to sprout with young barley, growing up from barley corn which the 'croppies' had carried in their pockets to eat while on the march. The oblique implication was that the seeds of violent resistance sowed in the Year of Liberty had flowered in what Yeats called "the right rose tree" of 1916. I did not realize at the time that the original heraldic murderous encounter between Protestant yeoman and Catholic rebel was to be initiated again in the summer of 1969, in Belfast, two months after the book was published.[11]

Heaney speaks in the poem as one of the "fatal conclave", a more effective strategy than his use of the Commander's voice as a semi-ironic filter. However, in 'Bogland', a threshold-poem like 'The Tollund Man' ("I wrote it quickly . . . revised it on the hoof"[12]), he abandons both straight history and the dramatic monologue. He opens his proper door into "the matter of Ireland", by imagining history as an experience rather than a chain of events, by dramatising his own imaginative experience of history, by discovering within his home-ground a myth that fits the inconclusiveness both of memory and of Irish history, and by fusing the psychic self-searching of poet and nation:

> Our pioneers keep striking
> Inwards and downwards . . .

1969 thus coincided with Heaney's readiness to pioneer the frontiers of Irish consciousness: "From that moment the problems of poetry moved from being simply a matter of achieving the satisfactory verbal icon to being a search for images and symbols adequate to our predicament". Again, "those language and place-names . . . poems [in *Wintering Out*] politicize the terrain and the imagery of the first two books."[13] The poem that most literally, and perhaps most richly, "politicizes the terrain" is 'The Other Side', in which Heaney intertwines land, religion, and language to characterise, and tentatively close, the distance between his own family and a neighbouring Protestant farmer:

> I lay where his lea sloped
> to meet our fallow,
> nested on moss and rushes,
>
> my ear swallowing
> his fabulous, biblical dismissal,
> that tongue of chosen people.

The "Inwards and downwards" thrust of *Wintering Out* also draws Heaney "into [the] trail" of anonymous ancestors, still more deprived: servant boy, mummer (though this model of the vanishing tribal artist has British origins), mound-dwellers, "geniuses who creep/'out of every corner/of the woodes and glennes' ". A third strike opens up a new and crucial terrain: contemporary Belfast, implicit landscape of 'A Northern Hoard'. This sequence puts the question to which the surrounding poems probe answers: "What do I say if they wheel out their dead?". 'Tinder', whose prehistoric imagery connects with that of 'The Tollund Man', might be described as Heaney's 'Easter 1916'. But his then-and-now contrast displays little even of Yeats's qualified excitement. The underprivileged "tribe" who have lit the tinder of revolution, wonder what to do with their "new history", while the poet simultaneously wonders about his role:

> Now we squat on cold cinder,
> Red-eyed, after the flames' soft thunder
>
> And our thoughts settle like ash.
> We face the tundra's whistling brush. . . .

Finally, in the "language and place-names" poems—which pioneer the kind of resonance that Edward Thomas, contrastingly, released—Heaney finds a role within his own profession. A unique brand of revolutionary action, linguistic decolonisation, takes on the English language itself, with mixed declarations of love and war:

> But now our river tongues must rise
> From licking deep in native haunts
> To flood, with vowelling embrace,
> Demesnes staked out in consonants.
>   'A New Song'

As a group the poems insinuate that the ghost of Gaelic, local idiom, the sound of the land itself, all united in Heaney's own utterance, are compelling the tradition of Shakespeare and Spenser to go native.

He puts this, and other things, more bluntly in part II of *North*:

> Ulster was British, but with no rights on
> The English lyric

—or so they thought. Perhaps Heaney's poetry was always a form of revolution, like negro jazz:

> Between my finger and my thumb
> The squat pen rests; snug as a gun.

In Berkeley (1970-71) he became aware "that poetry was a force, almost a mode of power, certainly a mode of resistance."[14] To Seamus Deane he says: "I think that my own poetry is a kind of slow, obstinate, papish burn, emanating from the ground I was brought up on."[15] ("Obstinate" is a favourite and favourable word of Heaney's, signifying the immovable object or objection that reverses "No Surrender".) Up to and including *Wintering Out* his poetry may have been poetry-as-protest or protest-as-poetry in an extraordinarily profound sense: unjust Ulster hurt him into poetry. However, in *North* this subtext whereby Heaney makes up for the lost time of those lost "geniuses", the mute inglorious Spensers, coarsens as it becomes text. 'The Ministry of Fear' and 'Freedman' turn the tables with too much relish for the effect to be wholly ironic:

> Those hobnailed boots from beyond the mountain
> Were walking, by God, all over the fine
> Lawns of elocution. . . .
>
> Then poetry arrived in that city—
> I would abjure all cant and self-pity—
> And poetry wiped my brow and sped me.
> Now they will say I bite the hand that fed me.

Such speaking-out by the "slightly aggravated young Catholic male", or poet, accords with Heaney's view elsewhere in part II, that artificial balance distorts: " 'One side's as bad as the other,' never worse" ('Whatever You Say Say Nothing'). Much of the aggravation continues as a portrait of the artist, especially in the sequence 'Singing School' which begins with 'The Ministry of Fear'. The third poem, 'Orange Drums, Tyrone, 1966', was written before The

Troubles—a paradigm of how throughout *North* Heaney's creative maturity catches up on his youthful pieties and impieties. Combining aural and visual menace, the drums define Unionist hegemony in terms of "giant tumours", of a claustrophobic violence that afflicts its inflictor:

> The pigskin's scourged until his knuckles bleed.
> The air is pounding like a stethoscope.

'A Constable Calls' (2) lacks the same ultimate impact, the caller's bike becoming, even from the child's eye view, an implausibly melodramatic time-bomb: "His boot pushed off/And the bicycle ticked, ticked, ticked." However, both poems explore their own subjects; we infer the effect on Heaney's developing sensibility. 'The Ministry of Fear' and 'Summer 1969' (4) seem written largely for the sake of the sequence, and to fill in a poetic curriculum vitae (down to the provision of dates). Again, the nods to Yeats and Wordsworth in Heaney's titles and epigraphs (one of which is "Fair seedtime had my soul") look self-conscious as well as satirical. 'The Ministry of Fear' veers from the sharply specific:

> In the first week
> I was so homesick I couldn't even eat
> The biscuits left to sweeten my exile.
> I threw them over the fence one night
> In September 1951 . . .

to the archly literary: "It was an act/Of stealth." Heaney's theme may contrast the boy and the "sophisticated" author ("Here's two on's are sophisticated"), but his language need not divide them. Also sophisticated, 'Summer 1969' forces home-thoughts from Spain: "stinks from the fishmarket/Rose like the reek off a flaxdam"; cites Lorca and Goya as exemplars in the context of trying "to touch the people"; and finally applies too much local colour to the latter's portrait:

> He painted with his fists and elbows, flourished
> The stained cape of his heart as history charged.

This is elementary stuff from the proven matador of *Wintering Out*.

The two remaining poems, 'Fosterage' (5) and 'Exposure' (6), withdraw towards the centre of Heaney's own art. The former quotes the anti-heroic advice of Ulster short-story writer Michael McLaverty ("Don't have the veins bulging in your biro"), although the manner and content of the last line partially disregard it: "and sent me out, with words/Imposing on my tongue like obols." 'Exposure' (to which I shall return) sets up a much more genuine inner conflict than 'Summer 1969', and falls a long way short of confidently identifying the artist with the man of action:

> I walk through damp leaves,
> Husks, the spent flukes of autumn,
>
> Imagining a hero
> On some muddy compound,
> His gift like a slingstone
> Whirled for the desperate.

This truly is the doubtful mood and mode of Yeats's 'Meditations in Time of Civil War':

> I turn away and shut the door, and on the stair
> Wonder how many times I could have proved my worth
> In something that all others understand or share.

But if 'Exposure' casts second thoughts back over *North* as a whole, most of part II underwrites part I—in the sense of paraphrase as well as of explaining its motivation. A few critics have indeed found Heaney's personal and documentary explicitness more to their taste than the mythic approach of part I. Colin Falck considers it "a relief . . . that he can still call on some of his old directness in dealing with the Ulster conflicts."[16] But is the "directness" of 'Whatever You Say Say Nothing' either equal or equivalent to the sensuous immediacy of Heaney's first three books?

> The times are out of joint
> But I incline as much to rosary beads
>
> As to the jottings and analyses
> Of politicians and newspapermen
> Who've scribbled down the long campaign from gas
> And protest to gelignite and sten,
>
> Who proved upon their pulses 'escalate',
> 'Backlash' and 'crack down', 'the provisional wing',
> 'Polarization' and 'long-standing hate'.
> Yet I live here, I live here too, I sing,
>
> Expertly civil tongued with civil neighbours
> On the high wires of first wireless reports,
> Sucking the fake taste, the stony flavours
> Of those sanctioned, old, elaborate retorts:

'Oh, it's disgraceful, surely, I agree,'
'Where's it going to end?' 'It's getting worse'. . . .

Heaney too seems to practise a kind of shorthand: "gas/And protest to gelignite and sten" cannot be offloaded on to "newspapermen", while "the provisional wing" is a hasty reference that carries its own "backlash". His subsequent anatomy of Ulster evasiveness ("Smoke-signals are loud-mouthed compared with us . . ./O land of password, handgrip, wink and nod,/Of open minds as open as a trap"), labours the point in comparison with Derek Mahon's bleak earlier indictment:

> [We] yield instead to the humorous formulae,
> The spurious mystery in the knowing nod.
> Or we keep sullen silence in light and shade,
> Rehearsing our astute salvations under
> The cold gaze of a sanctimonious God.[17]

The mood of Heaney's poem comes over as irritation, impatience, rather than grand indignation (perhaps partly a result of his difficult gear change from poetic smoke-signaller to loud-speaker). The concluding vision of a petty society leaves a sour taste, because it admits empathy but excludes sympathy: "Coherent miseries, a bite and sup,/We hug our little destiny again." His blanket dismissal of cliché is more palatable, indeed a cliché itself. Yet it may have something to do with the fact that Heaney's own poetry—unlike, say, MacNeice's *Autumn Journal*—has among its many rich resources no means of accommodating, transforming, criticising such idiom. The inadequacy of media jargon, or of everyday commonplace, invalidates neither the political process nor "civilized outrage". However, 'Whatever You Say Say Nothing'—which Heaney did not include in his *Selected Poems*—essentially voices the same sentiment as Edward Thomas's 'This is No Case of Petty Right or Wrong'. Just as Thomas during the First World War insisted on expressing England in his own way ("I hate not Germans, nor grow hot/With love of Englishmen, to please newspapers"), so Heaney is justifying the language, aesthetic and perspective of the greater part of his book.

The lecture 'Feeling into Words', from which I have already quoted, coincided with the completion of *North*. By "a search for images and symbols adequate to our predicament", Heaney

[does] not mean liberal lamentation that citizens should feel compelled to murder one another or deploy their different military
arms over the matter of nomenclatures such as British or Irish. I do
not mean public celebrations or execrations of resistance or atrocity—although there is nothing necessarily unpoetic about such
celebration, if one thinks of Yeats's 'Easter 1916'. I mean that I
felt it imperative to discover a field of force in which, without
abandoning fidelity to the processes and experience of poetry . . .
it would be possible to encompass the perspectives of a humane
reason and at the same time to grant the religious intensity of the
violence its deplorable authenticity and complexity. And when I
say religious, I am not thinking simply of the sectarian division.
To some extent the enmity can be viewed as a struggle between
the cults and devotees of a god and goddess. There is an indigenous territorial numen, a tutelar of the whole island, call her
Mother Ireland, Kathleen Ni Houlihan, the poor old woman, the
Shan Van Vocht, whatever; and her sovereignty has been temporarily usurped or infringed by a new male cult whose founding
fathers were Cromwell, William of Orange and Edward Carson,
and whose godhead is incarnate in a rex or caesar resident in a
palace in London. What we have is the tail-end of a struggle in a
province between territorial piety and imperial power.

Now I realize that this idiom is remote from the agnostic world
of economic interest whose iron hand operates in the velvet glove
of 'talks between elected representatives', and remote from the
political manoeuvres of power-sharing; but it is not remote from
the psychology of the Irishmen and Ulstermen who do the killing,
and not remote from the bankrupt psychology and mythologies
implicit in the terms Irish Catholic and Ulster Protestant. The
question, as ever, is "How with this rage shall beauty hold a
plea?" And my answer is, by offering "befitting emblems of
adversity".[18]

My contention will be that "this idiom" can represent as unreal an
extreme as the other: that part I of *North* (unlike *Wintering Out*) often
falls between the stools of poetry and politics instead of building a
mythic bridge.

After the passage quoted above, Heaney tells how he found "befitting emblems" in P. V. Glob's *The Bog People*, and swore his vow
to the Tollund Man. What is the precise "emblematic" relevance of
these mummified figures to the "man-killing parishes" of Northern
Ireland? The prototype developed by 'The Tollund Man' is a
scapegoat, privileged victim and ultimately Christ-surrogate, whose

death and bizarre resurrection might redeem, or symbolise redemption for,

> The scattered, ambushed
> Flesh of labourers,
> Stockinged corpses
> Laid out in the farmyards. . . .

Here Heaney alludes particularly to Catholic victims of sectarian murder in the nineteen-twenties. His comment to James Randall interprets the amount of family as well as religious feeling in the poem: "The Tollund Man seemed to me like an ancestor almost, one of my old uncles, one of those moustached archaic faces you used to meet all over the Irish countryside."[19] Thus related to "the moustached/dead, the creel-fillers" elsewhere in *Wintering Out*, the Man becomes the logical conclusion, the terminal case, the *reductio* of ancestral dispossession and oppression. In 'Feeling into Words', having summarised Glob's account of "ritual sacrifices to the Mother Goddess" for the sake of fertility, Heaney asserts: "Taken in relation to the tradition of Irish political martyrdom for that cause whose icon is Kathleen ni Houlihan, this is more than an archaic barbarous rite: it is an archetypal pattern. And the unforgettable photographs . . . blended in my mind with photographs of atrocities, past and present, in the long rites of Irish political and religious struggles."[20] Heaney does not distinguish between involuntary and voluntary "martyrdom", and the nature of his "archetype" is such as to subsume the latter within the former.

If 'The Tollund Man' and its glosses lay down a "pattern" for *North*, as it seems reasonable to suppose, how do the later Bog poems compare with the original model? 'The Grabaulle Man' obviously invites such a comparison; even the inference that the poems typify successive books (after the manner of 'Sailing to Byzantium' and 'Byzantium', or 'Toads' and 'Toads Revisited'). Whereas 'The Tollund Man' varies its angle of approach and moves with the dynamic of a pilgrimage, 'The Grabaulle Man' has more the air of a set-piece, arrival, its subject celebrated because he's there, rather than summoned into being by the poet's need:

> As if he had been poured
> in tar, he lies
> on a pillow of turf
> and seems to weep

> the black river of himself.
> The grain of his wrists
> is like bog oak,
> the ball of his heel
>
> like a basalt egg.

A difference in quality issues from the difference in stance: emotion anticipated in excitement gives way to tranquil contemplation; the intensity of conversion to ritual observance; crucifixion to resurrection. Almost too dutifully the poem attends to wrists, heel, instep, hips, spine, chin, throat, hair—inclining to rosary beads indeed. The chain of inventive similes reinforces the point that the Man has been translated into the element of the bog, and is thus at one with faintly healing Nature, but the Tollund Man somehow remains the *human* face of the Bog People. The less elaborate physical detail in the first poem counts for more, especially "The mild pods of his eyelids". "Mild" combines physical suggestiveness with a subliminal reference to Jesus ("Gentle Jesus, meek and mild"), while its last three letters set up a soothing assonance within the line, which ratifies the union. The two humanising images in 'The Grabaulle Man': "And his rusted hair,/a mat unlikely/as a foetus's", "bruised like a forceps baby", compete with each other and retain a chiefly visual quality. (Again, the simple "stained face" of 'The Tollund Man' says more.) The climax of the poem, following on the latter simile, appears unduly self-referring, pointed towards the "perfection" with which the rosary has been told:

> but now he lies
> perfected in my memory,
> down to the red horn
> of his nails,
>
> hung in the scales
> with beauty and atrocity. . . .

Beauty on the whole has outweighed atrocity by the time we reach "the actual weight/of each hooded victim,/slashed and dumped". In fact the poem almost proclaims the victory of metaphor over "actuality":

> Who will say 'corpse'
> to his vivid cast?
> Who will say 'body'
> to his opaque repose?

Possibly someone should. The ultimate difference between the two poems is that between Christ on the Cross and a holy picture: the urgent presence of 'The Tollund Man' worked "to a saint's kept body". Heaney may have mistaken his initial epiphany for a literal signpost, when it was really a destination, a complete emotional curve that summed up profound feelings and wishes about the situation in Northern Ireland. The ambiguous resolution—"lost,/Unhappy and at home"—may be as far as he can genuinely go, and it resembles other reactions in his poetry to tragic circumstances. 'Elegy for a Still-born Child' (*Door into the Dark*), for instance, ends: "I drive by remote control on this bare road . . . White waves riding home on a wintry lough".

Heaney's contracted or "perfected" perception of the Bog People in *North* renders their emblematic function, as well as his poetry, less complex. If what was hypothetical in 'The Tollund Man'—the consecration of "the cauldron bog"—has hardened into accepted doctrine, do these later images imply that suffering on behalf of Kathleen may not be in vain, that beauty can be reborn out of terror: "The cured wound"? The females of the species also attain a "leathery beauty". For the girl in 'Punishment', the wind "blows her nipples/to amber beads", and the tone of love-making compensates for any deficiencies:

> Little adulteress,
> before they punished you
>
> you were flaxen-haired,
> undernourished, and your
> tar-black face was beautiful.

As women cannot be "bridegrooms", Heaney must find them a different place in the "archetypal pattern". The final moral twist of 'Punishment' has attracted a good deal of comment:

> I who have stood dumb
> when your betraying sisters,
> cauled in tar,
> wept by the railings,
>
> who would connive
> in civilized outrage
> yet understand the exact
> and tribal, intimate revenge.

This is all right if Heaney is merely being "outrageously" honest about his own reactions, if the paradox "connive . . . civilized" is designed to corner people who think they have risen above the primitive, if the poem exposes a representative Irish conflict between "humane reason" and subconscious allegiances. But can the poet run with the hare ("I can feel the tug/of the halter") and hunt with the hounds? Ciaran Carson observes:

> Being killed for adultery is one thing; being tarred and feathered is another . . . [Heaney] seems to be offering his "understanding" of the situation almost as a consolation . . . It is as if he is saying, suffering like this is natural; these things have always happened; they happened then, they happen now, and that is sufficient ground for understanding and absolution. It is as if there never were and never will be any political consequences of such acts; they have been removed to the realm of sex, death and inevitability.[21]

At the same time, Heaney does in a sense make a political point by endorsing the "idiom", of something deeper than politics. (Although today's anthropology may only be yesterday's politics.) Blake Morrison argues:

> It would be going too far to suggest that 'Punishment' in particular and the Bog poems generally offer a defence of Republicanism; but they are a form of 'explanation'. Indeed the whole procedure of *North* is such as to give sectarian killing in Ulster a historical respectability which it is not usually given in day-to-day journalism.[22]

In fact Heaney doesn't license the latter. He excludes the intersectarian issue, warfare *between* tribes, by concentrating on the Catholic psyche as bound to immolation, and within that immolation to savage tribal loyalties. This is what he means by "slaughter/for the common good" ('Kinship'), and by "granting the religious intensity of the violence its deplorable authenticity and complexity"—and, of course, no apologia for the "cult" of imperial power. 'Kinship' defines the battlefield in astonishingly introverted Catholic and Nationalist terms—O'Brien's point:

> Our mother ground
> is sour with the blood
> of her faithful,
>
> they lie gargling
> in her sacred heart
> as the legions stare
> from the ramparts.

If *North* doesn't cater for "liberal lamentation", neither does it offer a universal, Wilfred Owen style image of human suffering either. It is a book of martyrs rather than of tragic protagonists. Only 'Strange Fruit' questions its own attitude, challenges inevitability:

> Murdered, forgotten, nameless, terrible
> Beheaded girl, outstaring axe
> And beatification, outstaring
> What had begun to feel like reverence.

The frank adjectives capsize what has previously been rather a decorative dawdle of a sonnet ("Pash of tallow, perishable treasure"; "Diodorus Siculus confessed/His gradual ease among the likes of this"). They also capsize a good deal else in *North*. Heaney told John Haffenden: "['Strange Fruit'] had ended at first with a kind of reverence, and the voice that came in when I revised was a rebuke to the literary quality of that reverent emotion".[23]

'Bog Queen' has the advantage of dealing directly with the goddess herself, so that questionable behaviour on the part of her acolytes may be ignored. The female figures in the poems, perhaps understandably, bear a family resemblance to one another: "The pot of the skull,/The damp tuck of each curl", "My skull hibernated/in the wet nest of my hair"; "they unswaddled the wet fern of her hair"; "my brain darkening"; "your brain's exposed/and darkened combs". However 'Bog Queen', although over-amplified like 'The Grabaulle Man', renews that well-worn genre the aisling by presenting Ireland as her landscape, weather, geography, and history, and by pushing her "old hag" incarnation to an extreme:

> My diadem grew carious,
> gemstones dropped
> in the peat floe
> like the bearings of history.

Since this is the one Bog poem with true Irish antecedents,[24] it can begin with an apt analogue of dormant nationhood ("I lay waiting/ between turf-face and demesne wall"), and end with an equally plausible "rising":

> and I rose from the dark,
> hacked bone, skull-ware,
> frayed stitches, tufts,
> small gleams on the bank.

These lines, and the poem's clearly shaped symbol speak for themselves. But Heaney sometimes asks too much of his myth, as if all
"statement" has been shunted off to part II, as if "archetypes"
remain above or below argument. ('Punishment' suggests the contrary.) A number of his comments on poetry nudge it towards the
visual arts—a surprising development from such a rhythmic
prodigy: "the verbal icon"; "a search for images and symbols";
"The poetry I love is some kind of image or visionary thing";[25] "a
painter can lift anything and make an image of it".[26] The notion of
"befitting emblems" also requires examination. Their original context is section II of 'Meditations in Time of Civil War', where Yeats
defines the purpose of his art in terms of "founding" his Tower:

> that after me
> My bodily heirs may find,
> To exalt a lonely mind,
> Befitting emblems of adversity.

Yeats's "emblems" are the many facets of the Tower and of his
poetry as a whole. Heaney seems to regard a symbol or myth as sufficiently emblematic in itself: "beauty" pleading with "rage"
within the icon of 'The Grabaulle Man'—Man and poem synonymous—rather than through any kind of dialectic. Nor does the
myth, as the resemblances between the poems suggest, undergo
much evolution. Before the publication of *North* John Wilson Foster
said of the language poems in *Wintering Out*: "Heaney's conceit
(landscape = body = sex = language) and the way it sabotages
emotion leads him into . . . difficulties".[27] In *North* the addition of
= Ireland, of the aisling element, makes it still harder to determine
which level is primary, or whether they are all just being ingeniously
translated into each other. Presumably 'Come to the Bower'
signifies the poet's imaginative intercourse with his country, but
does the conceit do more than consummate itself?

> I reach past
> The river bed's washed
> Dream of gold to the bullion
> Of her Venus bone.

When England participates in the landscape-sex-Ireland poems,
Heaney's edifice and his artifice wobble. In 'Bone Dreams' the
poet's lady uneasily assumes foreign contours:

> I have begun to pace
> the Hadrian's Wall
> of her shoulder, dreaming
> of Maiden Castle.

'Ocean's Love to Ireland' overworks phallic symbolism: Ralegh "drives inland", "his superb crest . . . runs its bent/In the rivers of Lee and Blackwater", "The Spanish prince has spilled his gold//And failed her". Love poetry in political language risks even more than the reverse:

> And I am still imperially
> Male, leaving you with the pain,
> The rending process in the colony,
> The battering ram, the boom burst from within.
> The act sprouted an obstinate fifth column
> Whose stance is growing unilateral.

This poem, 'Act of Union', pursuing the parallel between sexual and political union, and between imperialism and maleness, casts the speaker in a role which fits uneasily. And the allegory could apply to begetting Loyalism as much as Republicanism. In any case, the poem hardly persuades as a man's emotion towards his wife or child "parasitical/And ignorant little fists").

Given Heaney's previous successful explorations of landscape, water, femaleness, what has gone wrong this time? His prose comments support the view that an obsession with stacking up parallels, has replaced flexible "soundings". And in the case both of sex-and-landscape and of the Bogland terrain, Ireland is the straw that breaks the poems' backs. The Jutland connection does achieve certain archetypal dimensions but, as 'Punishment' indicates, the moral and political ground beyond the self-contained emblem is boggy indeed. With reference to the process in 'Kinship', whereby the poet finds "a turf-spade" and quickly ends up "facing a goddess", Ciaran Carson points out:

> The two methods are not compatible. One gains its poetry by embodiment of a specific, personal situation; the other has degenerated into a messy historical and religious surmise—a kind of Golden Bough activity, in which the real differences between our society and that of Jutland in some vague past are glossed over for the sake of the parallels of ritual.[28]

Whereas 'Bogland' enacted the stages of the poet's thrust into the past, he now obtains ready access: "Kinned by hieroglyphic peat . . . to the strangled victim" ('Kinship');

> To lift the lid of the peat
> And find this pupil dreaming
> Of neolithic wheat!
>
> 'Belderg'

That exclamation (at quernstones) represents a kind of elementary archaeological awe, borne out by the poem's Irish, Planter, and Norse 'growth rings' which express simply "A congruence of lives". In *Wintering Out* Heaney worked from present to past, interpreting (the historic congruence and incongruity of 'The Other Side'); in *North* he works from past to present—equating. The book appears fascinated more by bones, fossils, relics, archaisms—"antler combs, bone pins,/coins, weights, scale-pans"—than by those things which they are emblems of. 'Bone Dreams', as perhaps its title candidly admits, loses all contact with the thing itself. "I wind it in//the sling of mind/to pitch it at England". An ecumenical gesture, despite the metaphor, but "England" soon becomes an amalgam of history, geography, literary and linguistic tradition ("Elizabethan canopies,/ Norman devices", "*ban-hus* . . . where the soul/fluttered a while", "I am . . . a chalk giant", "Hadrian's Wall" etc.). Apart from section VI, a beautifully exact poem about a mole—and moles do focus differences between the Irish and English terrains—the poem turns the tables on Romantic versions of Ireland in English literature.

But the real costume-drama imports into *North* are the Vikings. The title-poem begins with the poet searching for a kindred revelation to that of 'The Tollund Man':

> I returned to a long strand,
> the hammered shod of a bay,
> and found only the secular
> powers of the Atlantic thundering.
>
> I faced the unmagical
> invitations of Iceland,
> the pathetic colonies
> of Greenland, and suddenly
>
> those fabulous raiders. . . .

The somewhat abstract adjectival sequence—"secular", "un-magical", "fabulous"—gives the show away. Why not write a "secular" or nature poem about the sea? (Like 'Shoreline' in *Door into the Dark*, where the Danes are a notional and mysterious "black hawk bent on the sail".) Why dismiss Iceland as "unmagical", un-less because Heaney is not Auden? "Suddenly" (at the end of a stanza) introduces "fabulous raiders" to fable-hungry poet too much on cue. They also open communication with remarkable speed, and the word "epiphany", deeply implicit in 'The Tollund Man', is actually used:

> ocean-deafened voices
> warning me, lifted again
> in violence and epiphany.
> The longship's swimming tongue
>
> was buoyant with hindsight—
> it said Thor's hammer swung
> to geography and trade,
> thick-witted couplings and revenges,
>
> the hatreds and behindbacks
> of the althing, lies and women,
> exhaustions nominated peace,
> memory incubating the spilled blood.

This is Heaney's own "hindsight", a "relevant" historical sum-mary which hardly requires such elaborate sponsorship. (May he be forgiven the zeugma "lies and women"!). And does the idea of the North really provide an umbrella for the not very Nordic north of Ireland, fertility rites and capital punishment in prehistoric Den-mark, and the conquests of the Vikings in Ireland—coming to or from the north? Although all these different places, time-zones and moral worlds clearly strike genuine imaginative chords in Heaney, why attempt to unify them into a mythic confederation? Perhaps again in order to stress the obvious: "these things have always hap-pened", as Carson says, and as Morrison finally puts it: "His allusions to former cultures amount to a sort of historical deter-minism."[29] Yet determinism, the plundering of the past for parallels, circular thinking (all incidentally features of Republican and Loyalist ideology) once more insist on "territorial piety", on a religious-anthropological, even slightly glamorous way of appre-hending the conflict, beside which "talks between elected represen-tatives" indeed look dull. In the last three quatrains of 'North' the

longship adds an aesthetic to the subject-matter it has already
supplied:

> It said, 'Lie down
> in the word-hoard, burrow
> the coil and gleam
> of your furrowed brain.
>
> Compose in darkness.
> Expect aurora borealis
> in the long foray
> but no cascade of light.
>
> Keep your eye clear
> as the bleb of the icicle,
> trust the feel of what nubbed treasure
> your hands have known'.

This self-dedication hints at a purpose—"long foray"—beyond
"befitting emblems", and to which Heaney's sensuous intimacy
with his world ("nubbed treasure") might contribute a value as well
as an "explanation". Like D. H. Lawrence and Ted Hughes before
him, he edges towards turning his instinctive sureties into a philo-
sophy.

Ritual is undoubtedly a value and a method, as well as a subject,
in *North*. It sets and sets off the emblems. While of course aware that
some rituals have more in their favour than others, Heaney employs
the term a little oddly at times: "the long rites of Irish political and
religious struggles". A struggle is not a rite, just as murder like that
at Vinegar Hill is not "heraldic" when it happens. The decorative
tinge that Heaney imparts to violence and to history derives from a
ritualising habit, which itself derives from his religious sensibility.
The continual catalogues in *North*—whether details of the Bog
People, inventories of objects like "antler-pins", or historical sum-
maries as in the message of the longship—level disparate experience
into a litany, a rosary, a faintly archaic incantation: "neighbourly,
scoretaking/Killers, haggers/and hagglers, gombeen-men/hoarders
of grudges and gain". In those lines from 'Viking Dublin' alliteration swamps meaning. 'Funeral Rites' declares Heaney's love for
the positive function of ritual:

> Now as news comes in
> of each neighbourly murder
> we pine for ceremony,
> customary rhythms. . . .

(An echo of Yeats there.) Carson praises the poem's initial evocation of remembered funerals:

> their eyelids glistening,
> their dough-white hands
> shackled in rosary-beads

but then comments: "all too soon, we are back in the world of mega-lithic doorways and charming, noble barbarity".[30] The worthy root-emotion of 'Funeral Rites' is that of 'The Tollund Man'—Heaney's passionate desire to "assuage",[31] but he goes to such ritualistic lengths as to obliterate his starting-point:

> I would restore
>
> the great chambers of Boyne,
> prepare a sepulchre
> under the cupmarked stones . . .
>
> Somnambulant women,
> left behind, move
> through emptied kitchens
>
> imagining our slow triumph
> towards the mounds.

An affirmation of "custom" and "ceremony"—especially as a kind of mass trance—cannot in itself earn "the cud of memory/allayed for once". Heaney's "rites", ancient, modern or imagined, are pro-foundly "Catholic" in character:

> My sensibility was formed by the dolorous murmurings of the rosary, and the generally Marian quality of devotion. The reality that was addressed was maternal, and the posture was one of sup-plication . . . . Irish Catholicism, until about ten years ago, had this Virgin Mary worship, almost worship. In practice, the shrines, the rosary beads, all the devotions were centred towards a feminine presence, which I think was terrific for the sensibility. I think that the 'Hail Mary' is more of a poem than the 'Our Father'. 'Our Father' is between chaps, but there's something faintly amorous about the 'Hail Mary'.[32]

The sense in *North* that something is to be gained by going through the ritual, telling the beads, adopting a posture of supplication or worship, curiously aligns Heaney with the early rather than the later Yeats (the Catholic ethos of the Rhymers Club). 'A Prayer for my

Daughter', on the other hand, is not only a prayer but a contest in which "custom" and "ceremony" engage with their opposites.

The whole design of *North*, including its layout, proclaims a more punctilious patterning than that of Heaney's first three books: "I had a notion of *North*, the opening of *North*: those poems came piecemeal now and again, and then I began to see a shape. They were written and rewritten a lot".[33] In contrast with the fecund variety of *Wintering Out* there is system, homogenisation. Certain poems seem dictated by the scheme (rather than vice versa), commissioned to fill in the myth or complete the ritual. Conspicuous among these are three first-person quatrain sequences, all in six parts: 'Viking Dublin: Trial Pieces', 'Bone Dreams' and 'Kinship'. Neatly spanning the Vikings, England and Bogland, the sequences present the poet in a somewhat self-conscious physical and imaginative relation to each mythic territory: "a worm of thought//I follow into the mud", "I push back/through dictions"; "I step through origins". 'Land' and 'Gifts of Rain' in *Wintering Out* began this kind of open quest, which owes a debt to the Ted Hughes of *Wodwo*. But the further back Heaney pushes, in default of a specific impulse, the more specialised or specialist he in fact becomes; so that the sequences exaggerate the book's anthropological, archaeological and philological tendency. The evolution since *Wintering Out* of the theme of language typifies other contractions. The place-name poems, if occasionally too calculated, stir mutual vibrations between landscape and language. But in 'Viking Dublin' Heaney's phonetic fantasy drives a huge wedge between word and thing: a longship's "clinker-built hull" is "spined and plosive/as *Dublin*". 'Kinship', already off to a sign-posting start ("Kinned by hieroglyphic/peat") that has travelled far from "We have no prairies" ('Bogland'), eventually goes into a swoon of synonyms:

> Quagmire, swampland, morass:
> the slime kingdoms,
> domains of the cold-blooded,
> of mud pads and dirtied eggs.

> But *bog*
> meaning soft,
> the fall of windless rain. . . .

'Bone Dreams', perhaps because of the poet's outsider position, relies more heavily on linguistic keys to unlock England: "Elizabethan canopies,/Norman devices,//the erotic mayflowers/of Provence/and the ivied latins/of churchmen", "the scop's/twang, the iron/flash of consonants/cleaving the line". This comes uncomfortably close to the way Heaney talks about English in his lecture 'Englands of the Mind' (1976). In Geoffrey Hill's poetry: "The native undergrowth, both vegetative and verbal, the barbaric scrollwork of fern and ivy, is set against the tympanum and chancel-arch, against the weighty elegance of imperial Latin";[34] "[Hughes's] consonants . . . take the measure of his vowels like calipers, or stud the line like rivets".[35] That the gap has narrowed between Heaney's creative and critical idioms, while widening between word and thing, underlines the extent to which the artist's own specialism also figures in these poems. Every poet worth his salt imprints his poetry with a subtext about poetry itself—as Heaney does, profoundly and skilfully, in 'The Forge' or 'Bogland'. A minority, because of the particular nature of their art, go public like Yeats as the poet-artist, taking on all comers. The protagonist's high profile in the *North* sequences, however, reveals him almost incestuously involved with the contents of his own imagination:

> My words lick around
> cobbled quays, go hunting
> lightly as pampooties
> over the skull-capped ground.
>
> 'Viking Dublin'

> I grew out of all this
> like a weeping willow
> inclined to
> the appetites of gravity.
>
> 'Kinship'

(Compare: "As a child, they could not keep me from wells".) Heaney's appetite for abstraction has certainly grown: "ceremony", "history", "violence and epiphany", "memory", "dictions", "the cooped secrets/of process and ritual". Several commentators on *North* have headlined 'Hercules and Antaeus' as symbolising the different approaches of parts II and I. Mark Patrick Hederman follows up such an attribution with this analysis:

Hercules and Antaeus represent two different kinds of poet: the first composes his own poetry; the second is composed by his own poetry. The first is the self-assertive poet, the political poet, who has a definite vision of things, who chooses his style and his words, who decides what kind of poet he is going to be. The second kind of poet is he whom Martin Heidegger calls the "more daring" . . . because he works from the heart and . . . articulates a song "whose sound does not cling to something that is eventually attained, but which has already shattered itself even in the sounding . . ."[36]

The poem certainly dramatises a conflict in Heaney (amply evidenced by *Preoccupations*) between an instinctive, "feminine" artesian strategy ("the cradling dark,/the river-veins, the secret gullies/of his strength"), and an ordering, "male" architectonic "intelligence" ("a spur of light,/a blue prong graiping him/out of his element"). However, Hercules may be quite as responsible for the prescribed rituals of Part I as for the outbursts of Part II: telling yourself to "Lie down/in the word-hoard" makes it less likely that you have done so. Stylistic examination suggests that Heaney has upset his former complex creative balance by applying architectonic methods to artesian matters, by processing his rich organic resources into hard-edged blocks, by forgetting "They'll never dig coal here".

Heaney should have been the last poet to turn "the word-hoard" into a dragon-hoard: "the coffered/riches of grammar/and declensions". The burnishing by repetition of certain words is an allowable consequence of recurrent subjects; other instances serve the grand design, as in the shot-gun marriages of berg and bog: "the black glacier/of each funeral"; "gemstones dropped/in the peat floe/like the bearings of history.//My sash was a black glacier/wrinkling"; "floe of history". But repeated rhythms and constructions do more than words to reinforce the ritual or cement the architecture. Metre, the skinny quatrain, is the most obvious formal unifier: "those thin small quatrain poems, they're kind of drills or augers for turning in and they are narrow and long and deep".[37] The narrowness of the line, in conjunction with that of the stanza, makes immense demands on both local variation and overall rhythm, if prefabricated cadences are to be prevented. As Heaney himself said later, "The shortness of a line constricts, in a sense, the breadth of your movement".[38] In fact, the quatrain often falls into two iambic pentameters, each harshly severed at the caesura:

> Come back past
> philology and kennings,
> re-enter memory
> where the bone's lair . . .

It can dwindle to mere layout unjustified by stress or sense:

> . . . Is a love-nest
> in the grass.

The method really amounts to a ribbon-developed sentence where
the enjambement of line and stanza quickly becomes itself a convention, and the basic unit must be a phrase that will fit into something
more like a passive receptacle than an active drill. This form blurs
climaxes and by-passes terminuses, while also letting the sequences
divide too tidily into equal sections. Nevertheless Heaney stiffens the
backbone of the poems by drawing on the "alliterative tradition".
His comments on its importance to Ted Hughes interpret his own
motives: "Hughes relies on the northern deposits, the pagan Anglo-
Saxon and Norse elements, and he draws energy also from a related
constellation of primitive myths and world-views. The life of his
language is a persistence of the stark outline and vitality of Anglo-
Saxon that became the Middle English alliterative tradition. . . ."[39]
The "iron/flash of consonants" undoubtedly strikes sparks, as in the
dedicatory 'Sunlight': "the scone rising/to the tick of two clocks,"
but can also be overdone ("haggers/and hagglers") and pepper a
poem with hard little pellets, for which the Anglo-Saxon compound
word is the model: "Earth-pantry, bone-vault,/sun-bank", "oak-
bone, brain-firkin" (an empty interchange of levels). Consonantal
monosyllables are conspicuous—taking their cue from "bone" and
"skull"—especially those with an archaic cast: shod, scop, bleb,
coomb, crock, glib (as a noun), nubbed. Heaney's fondness for the
hard-ed ending as participle/adjective (often with a co-opted noun)
has developed into infatuation: "the tomb/Corbelled, turfed and
chambered,/Floored with dry turf-coomb"; "Their puffed knuckles/
had unwrinkled, the nails/were darkened, the wrists/obediently
sloped". Sometimes the participles seem to involve a shortcut as well
as shorthand: "the cud of memory/allayed". The ending of 'The
Grabaulle Man', "each hooded victim,/slashed and dumped", is
less poignantly precise than "the scattered, ambushed/Flesh of
labourers" and "stockinged corpses" of 'The Tollund Man'. Constant asyndeton helps to compress the pellets, but the conjunction

"and" sets up its own syntactical orthodoxy: "geography and trade,/
thick-witted couplings and revenges" etc., "ancestry and trade",
"pinioned by ghosts/and affections,//murders and pieties". The
prominence of paired abstractions in the Viking poems underlines
their anxiety to connect. Thus the form and sound of the quatrain
exert pressure on syntax and meaning to the point where "customary rhythms" may indeed take over.

And yet *North* is framed by three poems which avoid or transcend
such mannerisms. 'Mossbawn: Two Poems in Dedication' occupies
a truly timeless zone within which "calendar customs" of domesticity and agriculture innoculate against the more barbaric "rites"
to come. Two emotionally and rhythmically expansive endings emphasise how much Part I cuts down, and cuts out, in pursuit of "the
matter of Ireland":

> And here is love
> Like a tinsmith's scoop
> sunk past its gleam
> in the meal-bin.
>   'Sunlight'

> O calendar customs! Under the broom
> Yellowing over them, compose the frieze
> With all of us there, our anonymities.
>   'The Seed Cutters'

The first stanza of 'Sunlight' does contain "helmeted", "heated"
and "honeyed", but their varied physicality shows up "slashed and
dumped"; just as the last four lines show up the periphrastic sensuousness of 'Kinship': "The mothers of autumn/sour and sink,/
ferments of husk and leaf//deepen their ochres". Culminating a sequence of diversely rendered "customary rhythms", the subtle
chiasmic assonance "gleam"—"meal" dramatises the complete
subjugation both of "love" and the poem—and the poem because of
its love—to what they work in. These poems are Heaney's real, un-
ceremonious assertions of "custom" and humanity, his most
important refusal to let "human utterance" be flogged "into
fragments". Carson observes that in the opening of 'The   Seed
Cutters':

> They seem hundreds of years away. Breughel,
> You'll know them if I can get them true . . .

"the apostrophe works perfectly; we realize how Breughel's realism,

his faithfulness to minutiae, are akin to Heaney's, and what could
have been portentousness takes on a kind of humility".[40] Compare
the strained self-introduction to Tacitus in 'Kinship': "And you,
Tacitus,/observe how I make my grove/on an old crannog/piled by
the fearful dead"—this he doesn't know and doesn't get true.

From composure to 'Exposure', from sunlit suspended moment
or 'Grecian Urn'-style "frieze" to "It is December in Wicklow".
With day, season, Nature, the weather, the heavens all in a state of
exhausted flux—"Alders dripping, birches/Inheriting the last
light", Heaney wonders about the lasting usefulness of his own en-
terprise, why he sits

> weighing and weighing
> My responsible *tristia*.
> For what? For the ear? For the people?

Anguished dialectic, recalling that of 'A Northern Hoard', banishes
both the polished icon of Part I, and the top-of-the-head arguments
of the rest of 'Singing School'. The contrast between images of dripping, falling, darkening, "let-downs and erosions", and "The dia-
mond absolutes", dramatises a profound self-searching a "sad freedom", which goes beyond the aesthetic politics of 'Hercules and
Antaeus' into the moral and emotional priorities of the artist.
Fundamentally, the poem asks whether departure from Ulster, for
which the writing of *North* may be an over-compensation ("blowing
up these sparks"), has precluded some personal and poetic
revelation (akin to that of 'The Tollund Man', perhaps):

> Who, blowing up those sparks
> For their meagre heat, have missed
> The once-in-a-lifetime portent,
> The comet's pulsing rose.

In this poem Heaney earns the label he gives himself—"inner
émigré", inwardly examining his emigration—which conflicts with
another, bestowed not quite self-critically enough in 'Punishment':

> I am the artful voyeur
>
> of your brain's exposed
> and darkened combs. . . .

Is this objective correlative, or substitute, for an interior journey?

Heaney's move South between *Wintering Out* and *North* must
indeed have shifted the co-ordinates of his imagination: distanced

some things, brought others closer. In an essay of 1975 Seamus Deane found Heaney (and Derek Mahon) a-political in comparison with John Montague, whose *The Rough Field* (1972) had "politicized the terrain" of his native Tyrone: "it is in Montague, with his historical concentration, that this fidelity [to the local] assumes the shape of a political commitment".[41] Interviewing Heaney after *North*, Deane encourages him to "commit" himself: "Do you think that if some political stance is not adopted by you and the Northern poets at large, this refusal might lead to a dangerous strengthening of earlier notions of the autonomy of poetry and corroborate the recent English notion of the happy limitations of a 'well made poem?' " Heaney replies:

> I think that the recent English language tradition does tend towards the 'well made poem', that is towards the insulated and balanced statement. However, major poetry will always burst that corseted and decorous truthfulness. In so doing, it may be an unfair poetry; it will almost certainly be one-sided.[42]

("One side's as bad as the other, never worse.") This interchange logically, but oddly, ties in the espousal of a Nationalist attitude with divorce from "English" modes. The combination marks a step across the border, away from "vowelling embrace". Similarly, whereas *Wintering Out* was written from the perspective of Belfast— Co. Derry, Heaney's hinterland interpreting the "plague"-ridden city, *North* was written from the perspective of Wicklow-Dublin; and a broader Nationalism:

> I always thought of the political problem—maybe because I am not really a political thinker—as being an internal Northern Ireland division. I thought along sectarian lines. Now I think that the genuine political confrontation is between Ireland and Britain.[43]

The vision of 'The Other Side' is absent from *North*: "the legions stare/from the ramparts". The 'Mossbawn' poems (though not the learned debate about the place-name's origin in 'Belderg') prove the local textures that Heaney's panoptic view omits. 'The Seed Cutters' also shows how the English dimension of his technique lives on in a concreteness and empiricism reminiscent of nothing so much as Edward Thomas's 'Haymaking' (written during the First World War): "All of us gone out of the reach of change,//Immortal in a picture of an old grange". *Preoccupations* salutes the varied influences that have fertilised Heaney's imagination, and which render irrelevant the false distinction between "well-made" and "major" poetry, rather than good and bad. (No *real* poem is "well-made" in any limited sense; no major poem ill-made.) Heaney here seems to join ranks with Montague and Thomas Kinsella, who in different ways, and often too self-consciously, have stressed the European and transatlantic alliances which should be reflected in the outlook and technique of Irish poetry. The Deane interview epitomises the intensive pressure on Heaney, including his own sense of duty: to be more Irish, to be more political, to "try to touch the people", to do Yeats's job again instead of his own. Printed in the first issue of the magazine *Crane Bag*, it heralds successive, obsessive articles on the relevance of his poetry to the Northern conflict. Again, Deane sets the tone with an attack on Conor Cruise O'Brien (Hercules):

> But surely this very clarity of O'Brien's position is just what is most objectionable. It serves to give a rational clarity to the Northern position which is untrue to the reality. In other words, is not his humanism here being used as an excuse to rid Ireland of the atavisms which gave it life even though the life itself may be in some ways brutal?[44]

Heaney demurs ("O'Brien's . . . real force and his proper ground is here in the South"[45]); nor is he responsible for the conscription of his poetry to bolster a sophisticated version of Nationalist ideology: "an Irish set of Archetypes, which form part of that collectivity unearthed by Jung, from which we cannot escape."[46] But one of O'Brien's "clarities" is his distrust of the "area where literature and politics overlap".[47] If they simply take in one another's mythological laundry, how can the former be an independent long-term agent of change? *North* does not give the impression of the urgent "matter of Ireland" bursting through the confines of "the well-made poem". Heaney's most "artful" book, it stylises and distances what was immediate and painful in *Wintering Out*. By plucking out the heart of his mystery and serving it up as a quasi-political mystique, he temporarily succumbs to the goddess, to the destiny feared in Derek Mahon's 'The Last of the Fire Kings'[48] where the people desire their poet-king

> Not to release them
> From the ancient curse
> But to die their creature and be thankful.

NOTES

1. John Haffenden, *Viewpoints: Poets in Conversation* (London: Faber, 1981), p. 64.
2. *T.L.S.* 1 August 1975.
3. 'Speech and Reticence: Seamus Heaney's *North*', *British Poetry since 1970: A Critical Survey*, eds. Jones and Schmidt (Manchester: Carcanet Press, 1980), p. 103.
4. *The Listener*, 25 September 1975.
5. ibid.
6. 'Feeling into Words', *Preoccupations*, (London: Faber, 1980), p. 59.
7. James Randall, 'An Interview with Seamus Heaney', *Ploughshares*, 5, No. 3 (1979), p. 18.
8. Seamus Deane, ' "Unhappy and at Home", Interview with Seamus Heaney', *The Crane Bag*, 1, No. 1 (Spring 1977), p. 61.
9. ' "From Monaghan to the Grand Canal", the Poetry of Patrick Kavanagh', *Preoccupations*, p. 115.
10. 'The Sense of Place', *Preoccupations*, p. 142.
11. 'Feeling into Words', *Preoccupations*, p. 56.
12. *Preoccupations*, p. 55.
13. Randall, *Ploughshares*, p. 17.
14. ibid. p. 20.
15. Deane, *The Crane Bag*, p. 62.
16. *The New Review*, 2, No. 17 (August 1975), p. 61.
17. *Night Crossing*, (Oxford: O.U.P., 1968), p. 6.
18. *Preoccupations*, pp. 56-7.
19. Randall, *Ploughshares*, p. 18.
20. *Preoccupations*, pp. 57-8.
21. 'Escaped from the Massacre?', review of *North*, *The Honest Ulsterman*, No. 50 (Winter 1975), pp. 184-5.
22. *British Poetry since 1970*, pp. 109-10.
23. Haffenden, p. 61.
24. P. V. Glob, *The Bog People*, pp. 77-8. The body, probably of "a Danish Viking", was found in 1781 on Lord Moira's estate in Co. Down.
25. Haffenden, p. 61.
26. ibid. p. 66.
27. 'The Poetry of Seamus Heaney', *Critical Quarterly*, vol. 16 (1964), p. 45.
28. *The Honest Ulsterman*, No. 50, p. 184.
29. *British Poetry since 1970*, p. 110.
30. *The Honest Ulsterman*, No. 50, p. 185.
31. Haffenden asks: "*The word 'assuaging' seems a favourite with you; can you say why?*" Heaney replies: "It's possible to exacerbate . . . I believe that what poetry does to me is comforting . . . I think that art does appease, assuage." p. 68.
32. Haffenden, pp. 60-1.
33. ibid. p. 64.
34. *Preoccupations*, p. 160.
35. ibid. p. 154.
36. 'Seamus Heaney, the Reluctant Poet', *The Crane Bag*, 3, No. 2 (1979), p. 66.
37. Randall, *Ploughshares*, p. 16.
38. ibid.

39. *Preoccupations*, p. 151.
40. *The Honest Ulsterman*, No. 50, pp. 185-6.
41. 'Irish Poetry and Irish Nationalism', in *Two Decades of Irish Writing*, ed. Dunn, (Manchester: Carcanet Press, 1975), p. 16.
42. Deane, *The Crane Bag*, pp. 62-3.
43. ibid.
44. ibid. pp. 63-4.
45. ibid.
46. Hederman, '*The Crane Bag* and *The North of Ireland*', *The Crane Bag*, 4, No. 2 (1980), pp. 98-9. Quotation from a letter of his to Conor Cruise O'Brien, which continues: "Your desire to demythicize us is, perhaps, an impossibility, and one which can only serve to drive the 'reality' even more deeply and dangerously underground".
47. 'An Unhealthy Intersection', *Irish Times*, 21 August 1975; quoted by Richard Kearney in 'Beyond Art and Politics', *The Crane Bag*, 1, No. 1, p. 9.
48. *The Snow Party*, (Oxford: O.U.P., 1975), p. 10.

TONY CURTIS

A More Social Voice: *Field Work*

A More Social Voice: *Field Work*

I want to analyse Seamus Heaney's skill in responding to the challenge of events in Ireland, to consider the extent that his latest book exhibits a growth in his stature as a poet, and to judge the extent to which, over the last five collections, Heaney's craft has developed to match his vision.

Here is a poet writing in a politically volatile country, a community split by sectarian violence, ruled at times by martial law. In a review article on *The Penguin Book of Irish Verse* in 1972, the Irish poet John Montague suggested: "the final judgement on the new Ulster Renaissance may well depend on their ability to learn a style from despair: it is the last quarter of the Twentieth Century we are entering, not the Georgian first." Seamus Heaney attempts to come to terms with his role as a writer in Ireland, developing "a style from despair". Within a few months of John Montague's article his third collection had appeared. It was to confirm Montague's summary of Seamus Heaney's work to that point: "his work seems to me a ritual preparation as his lost rural childhood and the world in which he now lives begin to come together."

In *Wintering Out* Heaney continues his examination of Ireland, but now it's the old language of his country that suggests an approach. In poems such as 'Toome', 'Anahorish', 'Fodder', and 'The Tollund Man' he rolls the Irish words and place-names around in the mouth. It is as if he is weighing the language that history has left him with. But the dedicatory poem 'This morning from a dewy motorway' which precedes the collection proper proves to be one of the most important. The body of the book acts almost as a counterpoint to that sense of present despair:

> Is there a life before death? That's chalked up
> on a wall downtown. Competence with pain,
> coherent miseries, a bite and sup,
> we hug our little destiny again.

Wintering Out has only an oblique strategy for addressing the accelerating chaos of contemporary Ulster and it is in *North*, published another three years further on into the escalation of war in Ulster, that Seamus Heaney begins to make clear statements about the situation in Ireland. The collection is shaped as if he is feeling his way forward to such poems. There are many poems about early Irish history provoked and influenced, as he admits in the *Plough-shares*[1] interview, by P. V. Glob's *The Bog People*. The latent violence creates potent images for him. He needs to deal with them, for his position as a Catholic is complex. At the end of 'Punishment' Heaney's sympathy for the victim of a sectarian tar-and-feather outrage is cautious:

> I who have stood dumb
> when your betraying sisters,
> cauled in tar,
> wept by the railings,
>
> who would connive
> in civilized outrage
> yet understand the exact
> and tribal, intimate revenge.

The sisters are "betraying" the Republican, Catholic cause. The humanitarian perspective which one had come to expect from his earlier work seems to be withheld here. The "exact/and tribal, intimate revenge" is understood, appreciated—in the context, and it is *his* context too at this time; Heaney is left "dumb". The poet is sitting on the fence.[2] This is a tribal conflict, splitting the fabric of the society.

That notion of the "tribal" is a basic one for the poet's developing view of The Troubles. In a way the crude, irrational divisions of society in Ulster may be answered only by imagery, the imaginative leap of metaphor. The political, social realities are so grim in that country that it may need the liberating force of a language that takes risks. In my analysis of selected poems from *Field Work* I shall examine the nature of Heaney's imagery, the extent to which his language and vision engage the problems in Ireland.

'Singing School' strikes me as the high point of *North* and the most accomplished writing by Heaney at this stage. He is acknowledging the fact that he is now a mature, established poet; that being so, what direction is his poetry to take? 'Singing School' like the bulk of Heaney's poetry, goes back into the past to trace roots and establish lines of direction. Unlike the bulk of his writing up to this point, 'Singing School' comes to an unequivocal commitment that takes account of the particular circumstances of contemporary Ireland. The sequence of six poems which comprise it is prefaced by quotations from Wordsworth's *The Prelude* and Yeats' *Autobiographies*. This is obviously Heaney's tracing of his genesis and development as a writer. Here, the landscape of Heaney's earlier life in Ulster and Dublin is viewed in strictly political terms:

> Ulster was British, but with no rights on
> The English lyric: all around us, though
> We hadn't named it, the ministry of fear.

he says in 'The Ministry of Fear'. The inspiration of English literature is there, seemingly outside of contemporary politics, but Heaney's writing from this point will be merely suspended in aspic, a "Glut of privilege", if it fails to respond to the situation in Ireland. The time has come, he now realises, to "name it".

The final poem of this sequence is the most important expression of the slow process of politicisation that Heaney has been going through before the publication of *Field Work*. He, like the Yeats of 'Easter 1916', acknowledges the fact that he must now be a politically-committed poet; no mere observer of The Troubles. He is a Catholic and born into the tribe of Eire and the Falls Road. To avoid the implications of his birth and necessary loyalties would be to deny his ancestral being. For too long he has procrastinated:

> I am neither internee nor informer;
> An inner émigré, grown long-haired
> And thoughtful; a wood-kerne
>
> Escaped from the massacre,
> Taking protective colouring
> From bole and bark, feeling
> Every wind that blows;
>
> Who, blowing up these sparks
> For their meagre heat, have missed
> The one-in-a-lifetime portent,
> The comet's pulsing rose.

Field Work takes off from that point.[3] There's no equivocation now about that commitment: the questions have been asked.

Seamus Heaney is destined to work as a poet. His birth and upbringing he now feels confirm him in that particular role.

> Fair seedtime had my soul, and I grew up
> Fostered alike by beauty and by fear;
> Much favoured in my birthplace, and no less
> In that beloved Vale to which, erelong,
> I was transplanted. . . .

There's a certain pretension to that quotation but also there's no
doubt that Heaney is determined to match the political moment.
The quotation from Yeats shows him to be taking the road of republican awareness and commitment:

> He (the stable-boy) had a book of Orange rhymes, and the days
> when we read them together in the hayloft gave me the pleasure of
> rhyme for the first time. Later on I can remember being told,
> when there was a rumour of a Fenian rising, that rifles were being
> handed out to the Orangeman; and presently, when I began to
> dream of my future life, I thought I would like to die fighting the
> Fenians.
>
> W. B. Yeats: Autobiographies

At least, from now on, Seamus Heaney recognises the purpose and
the burden of his Catholic republican heritage. That said, the poetry
in *Field Work* renders absurd the characterising of Heaney as that
"well-known Papish propagandist" by *The Protestant Telegraph* in
1972. It may be that there is no middle path in Ireland.

*   *   *   *

Field Work is meant to be read as a book, a whole. The overall
effect of the collection is that of a useful structure, reflecting a unity
of purpose. Heaney is concerned to clarify his role in The Troubles.
He is in the position now of being assured of an audience and the
confidence which stems from that is evident in this book. Seamus
Heaney had been working out his necessary loyalties over the previous four collections and that took an explicit shape in 'Singing
School'. These new poems deal with present experiences and people
who relate directly to Heaney's life. Although Heaney doesn't
divide this collection into numbered sections as he did with both
Wintering Out and *North*, *Field Work* has a clear structure. There are
three groupings: ten poems follow the opening poem, 'Oysters',
then come the ten 'Glanmore Sonnets', and finally fourteen poems

with the title sequence of four pieces included. The collection up to 'Glanmore Sonnets' has five elegiac poems and the final section has one, together with the grim rendering of 'Ugolino' from Dante, a sort of elegy for the whole situation in Ireland. One should pay close attention to several of the elegies in *Field Work* for through them Heaney commits to record an often moving personal relationship. There is a cumulative effect too as one realises the number of people each man and woman must know who have died as a result of The Troubles.

The opening poem of this latest collection states a determination to act, to "eat the day" so that the "tang" of experience "Might quicken me all into verb, pure verb". The violent facts of everyday life in Ulster must now pass through Heaney if his poetry is to be of any use. If poetry is to be more than effete, ethereal, a luxury, it must not "refuse" but, rather, must "quicken". There's an urgency, too, about this coming to life. Oysters have been a common food for some cultures: at other times, in other places, men have gone to great lengths to secure them. Poetry now in Ireland must be taken and tasted: through the "deliberate" concern with language, its power to define an experience and extend understanding. Heaney wants to be totally involved in the act of poetry:

> Over the Alps, packed deep in hay and snow,
> The Romans hauled their oysters south to Rome:
> I saw damp panniers disgorge
> The frond-lipped, brine-stung
> Glut of privilege
>
> And was angry that my trust could not repose
> In the clear light, like poetry or freedom
> Leaning in from sea. I ate the day
> Deliberately, that its tang
> Might quicken me all into verb, pure verb.
>
>   'Oysters'

The opening image of the poem, "My tongue was a filling estuary", is clearly in a direct line with 'Toome', and 'North' and 'Bog Queen' from earlier collections. One can see 'Oysters' as the latest in a sequence of poems concerned with Heaney's art and the direct influence of his country's landscape upon his life. Heaney has indeed travelled South and the first poem in 'Triptych' echoes this:

Laying down a perfect memory
In the cool of thatch and crockery.
                    'After a Killing'

There are many indications in Heaney's writing that his personal,
family life is settled and a source of happiness for him. Images of
The Troubles, the problems of the country as a whole, intrude themselves into the context. There's almost a guilty feeling at the quality
of life he's leading, the oysters, the "toasting friendship". This
poem establishes Heaney's refusal to live entirely within that world.
The Romans savoured oysters because they had the crude military
power to indulge their "Glut of privilege". They had slaves. It
would be naive for trust to "repose/In the clear light" in contemporary Ireland: politics, power, violence run through all facets of life
there. Neither Poetry nor Freedom is to be found "Leaning in from
the sea". They both have to be worked for. The door into the dark
leads to a forge again, but now there's an urgency in that "tang"
and "quicken" and "verb".

Deliberately, that its tang
Might quicken me all into verb, pure verb.

Heaney means *his* all—mind, voice, body, spirit: poetry is the enactment of all the aspects of his existence. He desperately wants to *do*
something about Ireland. At the end of *North* he recognises "the
comet's pulsing rose": at the beginning of *Field Work* he sets out to
catch its power, ride its energy path. This image of light and energy
is a critical one for this collection. There is a new intensity of passion
in the book that builds on the commitment proclaimed at the end of
North.

Seamus Heaney makes it clear in his talk with James Randall,
published in *Ploughshares*[5] magazine, that he is conscious of the need
to adjust his poetic style to the ambitious task he has set himself.

I wrote a fairly constricted freeish kind of verse in *Wintering Out*
and *North* in general, and then in the new book *Field Work*, I very
deliberately set out to lengthen the line again because the narrow
line was becoming habit. The shortness of a line constricts, in a
sense, the breadth of your movement. Of course, a formal decision is never strictly formal. I mean it's to do with some impul-
sive things, some instinctive sense of the pitch you want to make.
And with *North* and *Wintering Out* I was burrowing inwards, and
those thin small quatrain poems, they're kind of drills or augers

for turning in and they are narrow and long and deep. Well, after those poems I wanted to turn out, to go out, and I wanted to pitch the voice out; it was at once formal but also emotional, a return to an opener voice and to a more—I don't want to say public—but a more social voice. And the rhythmic contract of meter and iambic pentameter and long line implies audience. Maybe I've overstated that.

The poet is setting out in his recent work to *involve* himself more directly with the facts of life around him in Ireland. In a way, the success Seamus Heaney has had since 1966 enables him to "come out" and proclaim his loyalties. The danger implicit in Heaney's current reputation is that he may overstep the mark. In 'Glanmore Sonnets' he sees himself again in the "hedge-school" but can't resist the comparison with Wordsworth:

> I had said earlier, 'I won't relapse
> From this strange loneliness I've brought us to.
> Dorothy and William—'She interrupts:
> 'You're not going to compare us two . . .?'
> Outside a rustling and twig-combing breeze
> Refreshes and relents. Is cadences.

Claims of that nature are more properly left to others.

Heaney is a member of a disadvantaged minority in the North of Ireland: he is a Catholic and a republican. Perhaps he needed to distance himself from Belfast to gain a perspective on the situation there. In the *Ploughshares* interview the poet says:

> The crossing of the border has a political edge to it because we were opting to go into the Republic. But I was quite content in a way to accept and undergo that political dimension because I have never considered myself British.

That sense of Irish nationality is a major concern in several of these new poems. In the poem 'The Toome Road' Heaney sees the British Army in their armoured cars as "charioteers": they are just the latest in a long line of conquerors. To meet the challenge of the political realities in Ireland Heaney has still, though, to write from the rural context which is his birth-right. If the move to rural Eire is significant in a political sense, then so are the incursions of violence into that landscape. 'Tryptych' takes off from that point. The three poems attempt to enact the promise which Heaney sets down in 'Oysters'. They "eat the day" by confronting the facts of life in Ulster.

That countryside which in the earlier books meant bulls and water-
pumps, furrow and forge, is now made to include icons of violent intrusion. The following poem 'The Toome Road' has Heaney meeting:

> armoured cars
> In convoy, warbling along on powerful tyres,
> All camouflaged with broken alder branches.

and there the poet is clearly "quickened into verb". The weight of
irony, of protest in that "warbling" drives the motion of the poem to
"Sowers of seed, erectors of headstones. . . ."

In 'Triptych' the lines are grouped in stanzas of four, without
rhyme, with irregular metre. This poetry seems to me to be
powerful, clear and committed: it shapes our imagination for the re-
ception of Heaney's vision. 'After A Killing' pulls us up abruptly
before images of Ulster violence that have an iconographic strength:

> There they were, as if our memory hatched them,
> As if the unquiet founders walked again:
> Two young men with rifles on the hill,
> Profane and bracing as their instruments.
>
> Who's sorry for our trouble?
> Who dreamt that we might dwell among ourselves
> In rain and scoured light and wind-dried stones?
> Basalt, blood, water, headstones, leeches.

The two young men are "hatched" out of the collective memory of
Catholic Ireland. The verb reverberates through the following lines,
blurring and re-shaping our vision through the subsequent statements. This violence is the legacy of colonialism in Ireland. The
repetition of "as if" carries the significance of these figures further
into the poet's mind and back into a shared sense of history. The
"unquiet founders" is an ironical understating of the greed and
cruelty of the centuries of English kings, the efficient, ruthless
genocide of Cromwell's army and the still-hot memory of the British
Army's notorious "Black and Tans". Such spectres stalk the land.

The most obvious symbol of the continuing tragedy of Ireland is
the gun itself. The guns are the extension of men; the men are
products of the gun. The presence of this pair on the hill sullies the
landscape, they profane its beauty, they warp all that is natural.
They are a "brace", a pair—the hunting term picks up the meaning

of "hatched" in the first line and continues to trouble the reader. Is there a sense in which such a sight, the experience of handling weapons could be "bracing" though? Of course.[6] The root of Ulster's violence goes deeply into the *need* for violence. A generation who lived by violence, who could only *live,* express their sense of nationality, find fulfilment, through violence was baptised in the Easter Rising and the bloody Civil War six years later in 1922. Confirmed, enlarged and revered as myth, the principle of violence lives in the land.

The first line of the second stanza is, again, heavily ironical. "Sorry for your troubles" is an Irish colloquialism, a common response of sympathy for another's bereavement. Heaney is asking: Who cares? The deaths in Ireland barely nudge their way onto the front pages of the British newspapers now.

It is impossible to be "neuter" in contemporary Ireland; the division into Catholic or Protestant sects is absolute and ubiquitous. One may "pine" for such an innocence, but it must seem as rare and unobtainable as an orchid. Still people try to live as "survivor flowers" of a purer, simpler culture. The last two stanzas appear to be re-creating these circumstances. The Heaney's have a stone house on the coast; the fruits of the land and sea are at hand. It may be possible to buy oneself out of The Troubles in this way. Then the girl enters their home with the fruits of the field emblematically arranged in her basket.

> And today a girl walks in home to us
> Carrying a basket full of new potatoes,
> Three tight green cabbages, and carrots
> With the tops and mould still fresh on them.

It is like a still-life. The consequent uplift of the poet's and the reader's spirit is charged with responsibility. The colours, the crisp soundings of "c" and "g" in the penultimate line, sharpen our senses for the ambiguous "mould still fresh on them". The fields of Ireland grow vegetables and gunmen.

In the second section the poet consults a 'Sibyl'

> My tongue moved, a swung relaxing hinge.
> I said to her, 'What will become of us?'
> And as forgotten water in a well might shake
> At an explosion under morning
>
> Or a crack run up a gable,
> She began to speak,

A sibyl is a seer, a prophet. 'After A Killing' reiterates the Irish dilemma: a beautiful country spawning ugliness and violence. Perhaps Heaney can consult the oracle for an explanation? His tongue, one of the doors of his mind, swings open, relaxes to receive insight through a prophecy. He asks a simple question to unlock a truth.

The images of change are portentous—an "explosion", "a crack run up a gable" (this last is reminiscent of Poe). Both are the repercussions of violence. They could be man-made, but both can be taken for signs of supernatural intervention.: the well-water is forgotten, but, shaken may clear and catch light; the house shakes too and the crack imposes new strains on the structure of the dwelling. Perhaps the break-down of order is necessary to a new vision? Something fresh may emerge from the ruins of Ireland. This image points to the conclusion of the triptych. As Yeats went to spiritualist exercises for new tongues, so Heaney's device in 'Sibyl' is transparent: the "swung relaxing hinge" admits Heaney's own rhetorical voice, "I think our very form is bound to change". The tone is rational, almost as if it were as professor addressing a class. The following line with its three bursts of fire shocks the mood into a tension: sectarian dog-fights, the siege, are religious, tribal ghetto sets against the walls of its neighbouring enemy. The Army, the street armies, conspire at their own regression. Ulster Man lumbers through the Six Counties: a primitive, a prototype, representing the loss of everything that civilized man has achieved.

"Unless"—the Sibyl introduces the image of salvation. For forgiveness to find its nerve and voice it must act through the human body—it must come into Being. The axle tree of Eliot, Yeats, Watkins is now in Ulster "helmeted and bleeding": a bold image which stretches into the surreal over the next two and a half lines. The strength of those elemental verbs, "green" and "open" drives the complexity of the buds' transformation into "infants' fists". Unless the "fouled magma" can deliver forth a bright generation, nymphs, resilient swimmers, what hope can there be? The image tails off into bubbles with the four points. Ireland is caught in a web of ocean oil-map sections. Like mainland U.K. the future is balanced on "single acquisitive stems". How brittle that makes them seem. Also, if the politicians and the media jam our sensibilities with concerns of economic survival and "progress" we will be distracted from deeper truths, the insights that are realised only through narrative and metaphor.

Heaney is fond of the metaphor which leads him to dig into the

Irish earth, through layers of history, language, and tradition. 'Sibyl' ends with a grim image of Ireland as a body torn open, its "entrails/Tented by an impious augury". What passes for religion is no more than sectarian hatred: there is no true piety evident. There is no comforting the Sibyl either.

'At the Water's Edge' opens with a set of ambiguous sounds: are the "snipe" and "the keeper's recital of elegies" examples of the "comfortless noises" described by the Sibyl?

> On Devenish I heard a snipe
> And the keeper's recital of elegies
> Under the tower. Carved monastic heads
> Were crumbling like bread on water.
>
> On Boa the god-eyed, sex-mouthed stone
> Socketed between graves, two-faced, trepanned,
> Answered my silence with silence.
> A stoup for rain water. Anathema.

On Devenish island Heaney senses that the place has lost its magic. The keeper gives a "recital of elegies". This is a mysticism for tourists; they hasten the decay of the masonry which falls on the water, drawing who knows what response from fish or ships. On Boa the pagan carving allows a more sexual, earthy vibration. There is a duality; the pairing of words for the effects of contrast and complement is a pleasing variation on the style and is a strong form for Heaney's intent. The see-sawing rhythm, and use of alliteration close the circle of the carving. The "god-eyed, sex-mouthed stone" may have vision, but communicates nothing, its sensual voice is stilled, petrified in the graves' socket. "Two-faced" has a double meaning: the carving completes itself, looks inwardly, without reference to the outside world; it is also unreliable, a false, outworn god. Like the "carved monastic heads" on Devenish, it is dissolving in water. Both early Christian and pagan beliefs are crumbling: they have no direct relevance for present-day Ireland. Heaney moves on from these visits at least knowing that. The hearthstone on Horse Island is cold; it is the dead, blank witness of events. Through the open chimney the army helicopter patrol clamps its grid of vigilance. It moves by "thick rotations". Again, Heaney is creating that sense of overreaching control by outside authority, of entrapment, which was evident in 'Sibyl'.

On the windowsill are: "A hammer and a cracked jug full of cobwebs," and the arrangement has a tableau quality, as if the tool and vessel were the base elements of all societies, the beginnings of civilized settlement. They are the male and female, the sense of belonging to a place, trees, water, construction and survival; they have the symbolic force for which Heaney has travelled. Everything in him is humbled: he is again in touch with the elemental, the basic possibilities of life. It takes his breath away, the simplicity, the idea of going back to basics and beginning again. The only prayer is for that: the ''infants' fists'' must bud and grow to grasp the tools. The second line of the closing stanza has all the excitement of discovery— ''How we crept before we walked!''

And suddenly, finally, the poem resolves itself by political terms: the slow, deliberate march of the last two and a half lines:

> I remembered
> The helicopter shadowing our march at Newry,
> The scared, irrevocable steps.

the steady progress towards action and effect, the confrontation with the helicopter and the shadow its presence cast over them. The Catholics march at Newry through their fear because there is nothing else for them to do. They have to realise a collective entity for themselves; they have to go out and be counted. There is no going back and the final line of 'At the Water's Edge' builds on and supercedes all that Heaney has traced through the triptych: the movement has been through observation to an involved questioning, to a final and ongoing commitment. These three pieces confirm Heaney's concern that his move from Belfast should not make him unaware of

> The once-in-a-lifetime portent,
> The comet's pulsing rose.

The way in which Ulster-based violence can permeate any aspect of life in contemporary Ireland is emphasized in the elegy 'The Strand at Lough Beg'. In such a politically-charged context, this poem is a notable achievement. The writing here rises above the vagaries of the current strife and invokes a profound sense of loss. The waste of human strength as each individual dies is the true measure of the tragedy being enacted in Ireland. When under his title Heaney quotes three lines from the first book of Dante's *Purgatorio* he is establishing clear terms for this poem. Ireland is to be likened to Purgatory, ''this little island'', and Heaney takes an elevated view, as if looking down on his country. What the quotation does is set Heaney the task of rising through the pain of the experience embodied in the poem and establishing a longer perspective, one that contains hope, transcendence even. The strength of this quotation is that it directs both the poet and the reader.

The poem opens by establishing the setting of the action. The "White glow of filling stations" and the "few lonely streetlamps" create a sense of foreboding; Colum McCartney is leaving the banal, secure country town to climb away up into the hills. He takes "a high, bare pilgrim's track' . . . "out beneath the stars". It seems that the further this man drives from the town the more he divorces himself from safety and the known. As with the victim in 'Casualty' Colum McCartney wanders out of his "tribal" area at his peril. He enters the country of the Sweeney myth of old Ireland and the nightmare engulfs him. Violence here is legend and Colum McCartney is unknowingly re-enacting a cycle of pursuit and sacrifice. The terrorists' road-block blazes up in the road, faked red lights, faked authority, "dog's eyes" from the hooded heads.

The sense of a familiar, supportive landscape with which the first section ends is both developed and undercut by detail in the second movement of the poem. There were guns in Colum McCartney's experience. Heaney softens the effect of that first line, by making them "duck shooters", but by placing "haunted" at the beginning of the third line he introduces a threatening portent which colours "the marigolds and bullrushes" and prepares us for the "scared" of the following line, and the fifth line, the most striking of the poem. Heaney's timing is perfect: "Acrid, brassy, genital, ejected". The rhythm is a gun-burst, a short, clipped-off listing of qualities. They clash with each other within the line, a bitter smell, a seductive glint in the light, seeding there amidst the plants. The words grate in the ear; this is an intrusion. It's a phallic penetration of the land, a reminder of macho pressures, a sexual distortion of values. One's eyes and ears go over the end of that line to land softly on the following image of calm. We are returned to the pace of the farm by the line's length and rhythm.

The third section draws the reader into an exploration of that farming life. We are presented with two sentences that take us uneventfully into the middle of the stanza. Five of the first six lines have end-rhymes and the apparently calm, pastoral mood of the opening has no real hint of the impending tragedy until the alliterative *d*s of the fifth line. The "strand" is Colum McCartney's land, but the connotations multiply—his life is a temporal strand running through the world; it is also his hold on life; his life is one of the strands that, woven, makes up a family, a nation. The cattle float weightlessly on the "early mist" like ships, their eyes neutral witness to what at first seems to be two men, Heaney and Colum McCartney approaching at milking time in the early morning. The comparison of Lough Beg with a deceptively sharpened knife is a threatening to that pastoral scene. At this point the section takes off with an imaginative drive towards the resolution of its closing image. The long sweep of the next sentence, over five and a half lines, carries us much further than we could have guessed. The scene is not the distant past, then, Heaney's vision of Colum McCartney's death is in the present tense; it continues through the poet's life. The pastoral setting is made to contain the outrage of this man's mutilation and death. And right at the end Heaney clarifies precisely his relationship with the subject of the poem, his cousin.

This sentence has such an evocative power: the men were "sweeping" through the "sedge/Drowning in dew"; the ugliness of "blood and roadside muck" is salved by Heaney's kneeling before the battered body of his cousin and taking from the full, wet grass the cold, cleansing dew. The final rhyme of "dew" with "you" clasps the sense of the image. "Dab" is the perfect verb here: it's colloquial and tender. The moss has an ethereal quality, as light as air. There are obvious associations with the laying out of Christ at this point. The green rushes are the appropriate decoration for Colum McCartney in death: his memorial is the strand at Lough Beg, the renewal of shoots, coming green and green over again. Finally, the rhyming of "shroud" with "cloud" emphasises the sense in which this place has absorbed the dead farmer.

I regard this poem as the high point of *Field Work*. Heaney has been struggling to come to terms with The Troubles in his last two collections. He shows in 'The Strand at Lough Beg' that he, already the proven master of images from his native rural countryside, can build on that facility, deepening and extending his art to tragic proportions. However, the poem which follows, 'A Postcard from North Antrim: In Memory of Sean Armstrong' is disappointingly unresolved. It never rises above the basic desire to record another loss in a pointless random sectarian reprisal. But the next poem 'Casualty' is an elegy of a different order.

Although the victim of this bomb-attack remains unnamed in the poem (Heaney names him as Louis O'Neill in the *Ploughshares* interview) a firmer sense of involvement emerges finally. O'Neill was a regular patron of the pub of Heaney's father-in-law in County Tyrone, and the poet sees in this character an opportunity to widen the concern of his writing. At first sight there would appear to be little outstanding in this man, but the poem builds up the character of this casualty of the urban warfare in Ulster. He is one of the casually-reported dead and Heaney's purpose in the poem is to colour in details of the man, thus intensifying the sense of loss, the craziness of the violence.

The first section of forty-six lines maintains a regularity of rhyme that is basically *ababcdcd*. There is a sense of order in the description: the man is involved in the freemasonry of Irish masculinity. He participates as a fisherman and is a weathered practitioner of the true sport of the Irish—drinking. There is no pretence of social motivation in the pub or shebeen; he is a solitary drinker communing with the barman by a series of gestures. They perform a time-honoured "discreet dumb-show", a communion that celebrates drink itself. (One is reminded of Joyce's *Dubliners* and the habit of calling bar waiters "curates".)

The unnamed victim never becomes as important to the poet or his reader as did Colum McCartney, but one is, by the end of the first paragraph, already getting a sense of the man as a representative character. He has developed the tactics for survival as a working-class man in an economically-depressed country: "I loved his whole manner." Heaney associated with those tactics and one is reminded of the "old language of conspirators" from the earlier elegy.[8]

In the eleven lines of this section's closing paragraph the whole poem is put into perspective for the amiable drinker is killed in the backlash after "Bloody Sunday" in Londonderry. Even the violence is encoded in a bizarre way in Ulster. The slogan daubed in the streets reads like a soccer score. Heaney's "tentative art" moves us back in time to that week of bloodshed and multiple reprisals. There's an ironical link between the poetry as distorter of watches and the bomb's detonating mechanism here. The overall effect is one of taking that peculiar local colour that creates "characters" and outlining the nightmare quality of day to day life in Northern Ireland.

The second section moves us forward to the day of the funeral. Thirteen coffins blossom from the packed cathedral with a strange sense of beauty. Theirs is the beautiful still moment suspended

between violence and reprisal. It's a "cold/Raw silence", a knife-
edge, the wind catching at the priests' vestments. There's a slow-
motion effect; it could be Fellini. The sense of community, of
defence in numbers, by restricted movements, is born, and confirmed at the cathedral; its swaddling bands weld together loyalties
and a common cause is proclaimed. It is that deep-rooted refusal to
be held by a group cause, or to subscribe to its protective limits that
seals the man's fate.

There are two main aspects to Louis O'Neill's character as
Heaney sees him; for the man is drawn to the easy atmosphere of the
pub as a fish to a poacher's lure at night: "How culpable was he." It
is a measure of the madness of sectarianism in Ireland that the man
should die as a direct result of having broken "Our tribe's complicity". That is the crux of both the problem and the poem for
Heaney. He has to acknowledge the existence of the two "tribes",
and can even understand the reasons for such groupings, but the
awful, casual deaths from these bomb-attacks extend blame and
complicity to buildings and areas. The Shankhill and the Falls Road
might as well be different countries.

The second section ends with that challenging question:

> 'Now you're supposed to be
> An educated man, . . .
>
> . . . Puzzle me
> The right answer to that one.'

and one assumes that the final section will engage that problem. It is
to the memory of the fishing trip that Heaney returns: the funeral's
pace flows into that earlier scene. His heritage is to be found
amongst these working-class Catholics, "sideways talkers" takes us
back again to the "conspirators", "our tribe". The "dawdling
engine" has a calming, even numbing effect, it unifies and lulls the
funeral walkers as the act of fishing had linked Heaney and the dead
man.[9] As in 'Strand at Lough Beg' the scene on that day was hazed
over with fog. There are connotations both of threat and escape.
"hand/Over fist" in the "cold sunshine". Heaney says "I was
taken in his boat", he's almost passive, entering the other world of
the fisherman.

As the fish are hauled in a rhythm works each man to his "proper
haunt". This final section is all about rhythm: the rhythm of poetry:
the need for each person to find an underlying rhythm; the rhythm
and force of events beyond an individual's control, man determines

his fate in the distorting sectarian schisms of Ulster. The victim is killed by his own rhythmic, regular need to drink, to escape his home and enjoy the camaraderie of the pub. That pub atmosphere and the lough are variously his "proper haunt". He goes beyond Heaney's limits of experience and the poet ends with a plea for knowledge—"Question me again" reiterates the direct speech of the second section. In the context of Northern Ireland the dead have to pass some knowledge on to the living. The freedom Heaney "tasted" with Louis O'Neill—was it any more that a pleasant day's fishing, an escape from the city? The poet's task is to re-work such experience and test it in language.

'Casualty' records more questions than it can easily uncover answers. At this stage the poet is holding on to memories: an elegy performs that function most basically. At the end of this poem Heaney seems to be dedicating himself to the discovery of those answers. What is Ulster teaching us about human beings? At the lowest ebb, when one could be forgiven for despair, with such an arbitrary, casual dealing of death, the poet's task is to keep alive memories and to go over and over the facts of lost lives as Louis O'Neill's. It's as if the rhythm of memory is as purposeful as the act of fishing. Like Colum McCartney, Lous O'Neill returns to Heaney from the other side of Death. Both men carry themselves, heavy with dew, on into the poet's life. There are clear similarities with Yeats' '1916'.

For peace to return to Ulster the people have to re-establish the rhythm of the natural world. Heaney is pointing to the warped perspective of sectarian divisions as the essentially unnatural distorting force in his county. Ulster is sick: the people are being wasted by the cancer of violence. In *Field Work*, from 'Triptych' through to the last poem 'Ugolino', there is constant evidence of this. This book represents a clear progression from his earlier work in the way in which Heaney is trying to understand the events around him and practise his art meaningfully in that context. One thinks again of 'Digging' and 'Oysters'. Poetry works as positively as the gun, but on a different level. The belief that imagery and story can sway the imagination and alter the world is what drives every writer. In 'The Singer's House' Heaney emphasises the power of song.

> People here used to believe
> that drowned souls lived in the seals.
> At spring tides they might change shape.
> They loved music and swam in for a singer

who might stand at the end of summer
in the mouth of a whitewashed turf-shed,
his shoulder to the jamb, his song
a rowboat far out in evening.

When I came here first you were always singing,
a hint of the clip of the pick
in your winnowing climb and attack.
Raise it again, man. We still believe what we hear.

But to sing you have to rise to your feet and getting noticed in Ulster
may not be prudent.

In 'The Gutteral Muse' Heaney talks about the strains of living
and writing in Ireland. He portrays himself as "some old pike all
badged with sores." The poem's central image of "the doctor fish"
is rather strained though and the last three lines of the second stanza
work too flatly to explain the image. The pathos of the final image is
compelling however. Heaney seems worn by his experiences, he is
aging and detached from the "young crowd" who leave the discotheque. But he does hear in their "thick and comfortable" voices the
normality that is at such a premium in Ulster. The slime and thick,
viscous water that was so threatening in the early poem 'Death of a
Naturalist' is now restorative: "muddied night airs", "thick and
comforting", "oily", "slime", "swarmed and puddled"—the
sounds and movements slow down, salve the poet's sensibilities.
Heaney is attracted to the "girl in a white dress". We don't see her
or learn any details about her for she is at a distance in every sense.
He is, though, drawn towards the vitality and the force for life which
she represents. She is the tench. He gets no closer in the poem, as he
admits,[10] but the love poems in the second half of the collection show
Heaney very much swimming "In touch with soft-mouthed life".
The Muse is harsh, the poet "badged with sores" from a series of
losses in Ulster. Love, his marriage, and even such casual pleasure
as the discotheque's laughter at a distance, these things are a necessary balance to the strains of the man's vocation.

The 'Glanmore Sonnets' sequence is placed centrally in this collection and shows Heaney's most obvious attempt to locate himself
in the Wicklow landscape. He is also locating himself as a writer in a
specific literary tradition. The references to Wordsworth and to
Wyatt rather than Yeats, the choice of a sonnet sequence itself, these
are clear expressions of a need to draw on the strengths of main-
stream English literature. That comparison with "Dorothy and William" is the most direct indication that the move to Eire may

occasion a new phase in his writing. There's a sense of refreshment in nature, a practical realisation of Wordsworthian aesthetics: "Now the good life could be to cross a field/And art a paradigm of earth new from the lathe/Of ploughs. My lea is deeply tilled." Poetry there is an enactment of rural toil, "Vowels ploughed into other, opened ground,/Each verse returning like the plough turned round." But, as the plough returns to its starting point, isn't Heaney re-iterating his very first themes and images? He's still digging with his pen.

What is fine and superior about these sonnets are the moments when Heaney's language matches the emotional pitch of his feelings— elder trees fruit with "a swart caviar of shot"; across fields come "distant gargling tractors". This is no easy, pastoral idyll for there are constant threats from without: "Outside the kitchen a black rat/sways on the briar like infected fruit:" and what is primarily celebrated in these sonnets is not so much an escape, but, rather, a respite from the cauldron of the Ulster conflict. When Heaney counts the small boats sheltering from a gale-warning we are reminded of the passage from his essay 'Feeling into Words':

> I was getting my first sense of crafting words and for one reason or another, words as bearers of history and mystery began to invite me. Maybe it began very early when my mother used to recite lists of affixes and suffixes, and Latin roots, with their English meanings, rhymes that formed part of her schooling in the early part of the century. Maybe it began with the exotic listing on the wireless dial: Stuttgart, Leipzig, Oslo, Hilversum. Maybe it was stirred by the beautiful sprung rhythms of the old BBC weather forecast: Dogger, Rockall, Malin, Shetland, Faroes, Finisterre; or with the gorgeous and inane phraseology of the catechism; or with the litany of the Blessed Virgin that was part of the enforced poetry in our household: Tower of Gold, Ark of the Covenant, Gate of Heaven, Morning Star, Health of the Sick, Refuge of Sinners, Comforter of the Afflicted. None of these things were consciously savoured at the time but I think the fact that I still recall them with use, and can delight in them as verbal music, means that they were bedding the ear with a kind of linguistic hardcore that could be built on some day.

He does build on that "hardcore".

L'Etoile, Le Guillemot, La Belle Hélène
Nursed their bright names this morning in the bay
That toiled like mortar. It was marvellous
And actual, I said out loud, 'A haven,'
The word deepening, clearing, like the sky
Elsewhere on Minches, Cromarty, The Faroes.

(Sonnet VII)

The litany of names and places has always been important to Seamus Heaney. It opens for him a Wordsworthian "prospect of the mind". These 'Glanmore Sonnets' fixed at the core of *Field Work* establish an inscape as much as a landscape.

The love poems, or "marriage" poems[11] in this collection balance, complement and extend the book. The effect is not one of lightening, but rather of intensifying the reader's sense of the tragic by their contrast. That need to contrast, balance and repair is achieved most fully in 'The Harvest Bow', though this poem has been the subject of some heated disagreements: the Harold Bloom article in *The Time Literary Supplement* of February 8th, 1980, and the subsequent letter from Anne Stevenson, published two weeks later, raised varying interpretations. Like Anne Stevenson, I have always read the poem as an address to an older, rural figure. The details of game cocks in the second stanza, the fishing rod and the "Whacking" stick in the fourth stanza, are clearly referring to a man, a male mentor for the younger Heaney. The poet has confirmed my interpretation, adding the further clarification that the person addressed as "you" in the poem is, in fact, his father.

The firm impression is built up through Heaney's five collections that his family and friends are of central importance in the man's life and work. For example, *North* opens with 'Mossbawn: Two Poems in Dedication for Mary Heaney' and one would be naturally drawn to read them as being dedicated to Mary, his wife. They are, however, addressed to an aunt. The strength of feeling, the emotional force of the writing surprises when one first learns this.

'The Harvest Bow' is a tightly-wrought poem, its form complementing the central image. There are five stanzas of six lines, rhyming or half-rhyming in couplets. Internal rhyme and assonance are also used to create a woven form. Heaney is returning to one of his constant themes: the corn-dolly, the "throwaway, love-knot of straw" that represents his heritage. It twists and binds together the knowledge held by "Hands that aged round ashplants and cane sticks/And lapped the spurs on a lifetime of game cocks" and

sustains "their gift" which "does not rust". In the context of Ireland the sense of continuance, permanence, a simple strength, is
central to the survival of any real hope. There is a sense in which the
older man becomes the wheat. He can be seen as a John Barleycorn
figure, having acquired a "mellowed silence" over the years. The
poem has a simplistic but strong central argument: work with "fine
intent" and hark to your gift, others may then learn, "Gleaning the
unsaid off the palpable". There may be no easy, clear, instructions
from the previous generations, but Heaney and Ireland itself may
learn from what does survive, "the palpable". The pleasurable
sentiment of the memories in the third and fourth stanzas is realised
by the strength of detail: "Blue smoke straight up, old beds and
ploughs in hedges". The beating of his father's stick echoes the
concern with rhythm in 'A Constable Calls' and 'Casualty'. Here,
nothing is "flushed" out, there is no clear statement. Whatever is to
be said by his father is bound into the straw. *"The end of art is peace"*.
The quotation is from Coventry Patmore and Heaney told me that
he found it quoted "somewhere in one of Yeats' earlier books".[12]
On one level it is a glib Victorian motto pinned to a frail device. But
seeing the "spirit of the corn", becoming aware of the "burnished"
warmth of its passing, enhances, intensifies the "frail device". The
"love-knot of straw" is not thrown away; in a time which needs
symbols of hope the "drawn snare" is at least a record of a harvest,
it's "still warm".

The placing of 'The Harvest Bow' in this collection is important. I
see it as plaiting together the strands of the whole collection. The
"throw-away love-knot of straw" is a lasting embodiment of the
sun, the life-force. The poem rests on that paradox and brings about
its poetic resolution. What "does not rust"—there is a learned
silence held in the twists of straw; each bend and knot both breaks
and strengthens. Heaney is learning from the older man. 'In
Memoriam Francis Ledwidge' follows this poem and the
significance of the order is clear. Heaney is concerned with articulation; he's intrigued and excited by the possibilities of communication. The "golden loops" open out into visions: "I tell and finger it
like braille,/Gleaning the unsaid from the palpable". It is Heaney's
self-acknowledged task to knot these visions into language. The old
Man's "fingers moved somnambulant", without conscious effort
towards art; a skill that propels itself. The poet should, ideally, work
in that way.

The straw-knot tongue-ties the man: it is Heaney's task to articulate. "*The end of art is peace*" he reads in the symmetry of the "love-knot of straw". The corn-dolly has become part of his household. It mellows in its new context and gives out heat. It's as if the power of growth is held in "this frail device". The "spirit of the corn" may have slipped out from the knot, but the force of imagination can re-discover, re-create it there. Heaney's meditations on the harvest bow is both an unravelling and a weaving. The imaginative beginning of the poem is in reverse order to its progress down the page. The poet is taken to the genesis of the bow through its "golden loops". Like the love-knot, his poems will be no more than devices; but if they are successful they will be "warm" with emotion, the power of memory and "burnished" by its passage. Out of a crumbling world . . . ("old beds and ploughs in hedges,/An auction notice on an outhouse wall—") the poet has to make something, has to tie some sort of permanence into being. He has to find the strength as a writer to do that, for all his themes are brought together in this poem—the lost rural heritage, love, and the poet's art as a force in the real world.

The last two poems in *Field Work* develop this theme of the poet's worth in the world. In 'In Memoriam Francis Ledwidge' Seamus Heaney tries to explain the case of the Irish poet who was born in 1871 and died in Flanders in 1917. The story has an interesting complexity. Here was an Irishman fighting in the British Army at the very time his own country was struggling violently into being. "A terrible beauty is born" and Ledwidge is drawn away from Ireland to fight elsewhere. At that stage in pre-revolution Ireland he would of course have been a British citizen, and it's not so strange that he should die wearing the uniform of a British soldier. One can judge from this man's entries in *The Oxford Book of Irish Verse* that his poetry was very much of its time—he was a Georgian in style and spirit, and had obviously read Yeats. Heaney's interest in Ledwidge is related to the man's life more than with the work, except in so far as he sees in Ledwidge a sadly-missed opportunity. He too found himself engaged with events of momentous importance to Ireland. But Ledwidge remains uncommitted. Look at his 'Lament for the Poets: 1916':

> I heard the Poor Old Woman say:
> 'At break of day the fowler came,
> And took my blackbirds from their songs
> Who loved me well thro' shame and blame.

'No more from lovely distances
Their songs shall bless me mile by mile
Nor to white Ashbourne call me down
To wear my crown another while.

'With bended flowers the angels mark
For the skylark the place they lie,
From there its little family
Shall dip their wings first in the sky.

'And when the first surprise of flight
Sweet songs excite, from the far dawn
Shall there come blackbirds loud with love,
Sweet echoes of the singers gone.

'But in the lonely hush of eve
Weeping I grieve the silent bills.'
I heard the Poor Old Woman say
In Derry of the little hills.

That poem wants to become involved with the Easter Rising but doesn't employ the language to cope with the poet's feelings. The imagery protects the poet rather than illuminates the situation. Heaney's poem in turn seeks to examine Ledwidge's dilemma; he is a model for Heaney.[13]

'In Memorium' opens with Heaney's seaside trip to Portstewart with his aunt when he was six or seven. He remembers the fascination that the memorial statue had for him: the bronze configuration is out of time, its stance unrelated to the weather that day. The boy is perceiving the distinction between art and the world. That distinction is reflected in the metrical pattern of the first three stanzas; eight of the twelve lines are iambic pentameters. There is an ordered quality to the writing. However, the first line is irregular, as is the important "The loyal, fallen names on the embossed plaque". Heaney feels deeply the loss of Ireland. These dead sacrificed themselves for a foreign cause. That hollowness sounds out in the assonance of "loyal, fallen", and there is much play on words here to build up irony. The extreme Protestant sect in Ulster are, of course, known as the Loyalists; they have fallen from a true sense of loyalty to the Ireland in which Heaney sees them living; "embossed" reveals the falsity of the plaque's image, whilst it also contains "boss", the Irish colloquial term for a superior, foreman, owner, authority, even stranger. The State, in fact and in Heaney's mind, is prey to "the real winds buff and sweep."

The pilot, the courting couples, the farmer at leisure, create a holiday mood which wraps the young boy in a cosiness. It is at the nineteenth line that the use of "pet" again and the ripping barbed wire darken the mood.

The sixth stanza opens with a trochaic line and the four strong syllables of "Francis Ledwidge". Heaney is using the rhetorical device of addressing the subject directly in this elegy. What follows over the next two stanzas is a sympathetic description of a young Georgian poet—"Literary, sweet-talking, countrified"—a worshipper of nature for whom the wild flowers of May form an "altar"; who takes mass among rocks and who rightly belongs "amongst the dolorous/and lovely." The contrasting experiences of the following stanzas with Ledwidge "in your Tommy's uniform" are a shock. He appears unsuited and unprepared for the horrors of war. His "Catholic face" is haunted by misgivings about the morality of his position as an Irishman rather than as a soldier. He becomes detached from the realities of trench experience, a quiet ghost of a man whose body rhythms and spirit are more in tune with the "bloom of hawthorn" and the ancient burial chambers of Ireland.

It's not clear whether Heaney's aunt has any direct association with Ledwidge: I doubt it. It's enough that they are brought together by the memory of the statue in Heaney's mind. The device serves to extend one's sense of the unnatural placing of the poet in The Dardanelles and Flanders. Clearly, he should be "herding in the long acre." The first direct quotation from Francis Ledwidge's work confirms that. His premature and violent death "rent/By shrapnel" is in a sense more tragic than that of the forty year old Edward Thomas who was killed in the same year. Ledwidge was beginning to perceive the irony of his position. He was, though naïve, wrenched from the Ireland of the 1916 Easter Rising, both physically and in spirit: "I am sorry/That party politics should divide our tents." Ledwidge is, for Heaney, "our dead enigma", holding the issues of nationalism "British and Irish, in useless equilibrium". He sees in the dead poet the dangers he himself faces. Ledwidge has, in his naivité, followed "the sure confusing drum . . . From Boyne water to the Balkans". The Boyne, one of the most emotive place-names in Irish history, the scene of William of Orange's victory that secured the strong Protestant holdings in the six counties which form Ulster. And then the Balkans—the mistaken tactic that led to a military fiasco; the decision that haunted Winston Churchill for over twenty years.

At the end of his short life Francis Ledwidge misses "the twilit note". The poet is an instrument, but Ledwidge's natural key is that of the Irish flute, unlike the "true-blue" ones, the other dead listed on the war memorial beneath the bronze statue. The metaphor builds through the final two stanzas—"strains . . . tunes . . . drum . . . note . . . flute . . . sound . . . keyed . . . pitched . . . consort." That final "consort" is "sure" and "confusing"; what is Francis Ledwidge doing in a British Army grave? There's an echo of Wilfred Owen's 'Strange Meeting' here, and the poem is basically an anti-war poem. Heaney recognises that nationalism is the midwife of warfare and that the world lost a poet of potential when Ledwidge was added to the millions of dead in Flanders. Who can say but that Francis Ledwidge would have played a "twilit note" in the manner of the later Yeats? It is tantalising but pointless to surmise his return to an emergent Eire after the war and his growth from the poetic style of the Georgian first quarter of this century.

The present poem is, however, more ironical than Owen's 'Strange Meeting'. There's a sense in which Ledwidge too is consorting with the enemy, but they all wear the same uniform. The equilibrium, the levelling of death is in this case "useless". Ledwidge has missed the "confirmation" of Ireland. There's poignancy in that for Heaney. But also there's a sense that he must catch the moment, never again:

> . . . have missed
> The once-in-a-lifetime important,
> The comet's pulsing rose.

This poem is an important one for Heaney. More obliquely than 'Oysters' but just as positively, it makes a statement of intent. Heaney will learn from Francis Ledwidge. Over sixty years later he determines to reflect and influence events in Ireland in a way that the older poet never did.

It is significant that *Field Work* should end with the rendering of 'Ugolino' from Dante's *Inferno*.

> We had already left him. I walked the ice
> And saw two soldered in a frozen hole
> On top of other, one's skull capping the other's,
> Gnawing at him where the neck and head
> Are grafted to the sweet fruit of the brain,
> Like a famine victim at a loaf of bread.

It's a grim story and, unfortunately, is all too relevant to events in
Ireland. One may see the Six Counties of Ulster perched on the map
on the shoulders of Eire, under constant threat, so close to becoming
"the severed head of Menalippus". The poet watches horrified as,
mounted, his land eats off its own kind.[14] They too "consort now underground"—the connections with the previous poem seem firm.

> Is there any story I can tell
> For you, in the world above, against him?
> If my tongue by then's not withered in my throat
> I will report the truth and clear your name.

That is the challenge to the writers in Ireland. They are charged
with the task of reporting "the truth". In order to "clear the name"
of their country they must recognise the complexity of the issues: the
"tribal" divisions, the constant recourse of the British Army, the
pressures of economics and the demands of nationalism. Running
under all the public issues is the closed-circle of recriminations and
reprisals, a centrifugal force generating chaos from the core of the
Irish experience.

> . . . . for the sins
> Of Ugolino, who betrayed your forts,
> Should never have been visited on his sons.

That is all too often the case in Ulster: you are born fatefully into one
tribe or the other. The apocalyptic vision at the end of 'Ugolino' is a
terrible prophecy of Ireland's fate if a solution is not found to the
"monstrous rut" of the present strife.

Its effect as the closing image of *Field Work* compounds the
urgency of the book's main theme. 'Oysters' opens the collection
with a declaration of intent—the poet will "eat the day", consume
the reality of violence in Ulster and work towards a vision that will
match the depth of the tragedy around him. 'Triptych' points the
way further towards a sense of political reality in Heaney's reaction
to The Troubles, whilst the elegies that follow in the first part of the
collection express the constant sense of loss which attends those who
live in Ulster. Positive, human virtues are celebrated in the love
poems of the 'Glanmore Sonnets' and the poems that follow continue that celebration, though these are continual reminders of the
evil in the world, as in 'High Summer':

> on a warm ledge I found a bag of maggots
> and opened it. A black
> and throbbing swarm came riddling out

> like newsreel of a police force run amok, `
> sunspotting flies in gauzy meaty flight,
> the barristers and black berets of light.

One remembers "the fouled magma" inculcating in 'Triptych'. The vague horrors that one is brought to in the very early poem "Death of a Naturalist" are much sharper now.

> . . . .   The great slime
> Were gathered there for vengeance and I knew
> That if I dipped my hand the spawn would clutch it.

There the young Heaney has taken frog-spawn from the flax-dams but the final "vengeance" of the frogs is melodramatic. In the fourteen years that separate *Field Work* from that first collection the world has changed around Heaney. That's not to say that the earlier work is of less consequence, but the darker themes of previous books do harden and locate themselves in contemporary events now. There is a tragic dimension to this recent book that was no more than prefigured in earlier poems such as 'Punishment', 'For the Commander of the "Eliza" ' and 'Singing School'.

I see *Field Work* as building directly on the four previous volumes, and in this Heaney sets the model of Yeats before himself. He says in the *Ploughshares* interview:

> I think Yeats's example as a man who held to a single vision is tremendously ennobling—he kept the elements of his imagery and his own western landscape, the mythological images, and he used those and Coole Park, he used those as a way of coping with contemporary reality. I think that what he learned there was that you deal with public crisis not by accepting the terms of the public's crisis, but by making your own imagery and your own terrain take the colour of it, take the impressions of it. Yeats also instructs you that you have to be enormously intelligent to handle it.

That's the task which Heaney has set himself—to "deal with public crisis" by developing imagery out of his "own terrain". His poetry is now clearly committed to dealing with the violent situation in Ireland. Whilst acknowledging and defining his Catholic background, Heaney's poetry does take its base on non-sectarian, humanitarian principles. The imagery in this book engages the problems of Ireland as directly as anyone writing there during the Troubles. There is, of course, a danger implicit in Heaney's comments. By "making your own imagery and your own terrain take the colour of it, take the impressions of it," you are open to the danger of posturing as a public figure. However, I think Heaney unlikely to strike the senatorial stance of Yeats. He has, to this point, refused to wear "the great fur coat of attitude,"[15] though that could be a temptation, for the media picked up on the new book *Field Work* with alacrity; there have, over the last few years, been calls for writing that deals more fully, directly, with the Troubles. But Heaney himself has said, "to forge a poem is one thing, to forge the 'uncreated conscience of the race', as Stephen Dedalus put it, is quite another and places daunting pressures and responsibilities on anyone who would risk the name of poet."[16]

Field Work matches the hour in this respect, but on Heaney's own terms. The Troubles in Ireland, the involvement of the British Army again, the breakdown of democratic rule, these are highly charged subjects in the British Isles. Seamus Heaney's fifth book constructs an Irish landscape at once politically-charged, shared and relevant. At the same time it carries the considerable weight of personal emotion, grief and anger.

Writing of Yeats,[17] Heaney wishes that the *Collected Poems* had ended with "a kinder poem" than the "too male" 'Under Ben Bulben'. He would have preferred to see 'Cuchulain Comforted' as the final statement:

> 'Your life can grow much sweeter if you will
> Obey our ancient rule and make a shroud;

There is evidence in *Field Work* that Seamus Heaney has the poetic intelligence to bring to bear on the situation that in which history has placed him. He celebrates this "rite whose meaning is subsumed into song, into the otherness of art".[18]

NOTES

1. *Ploughshares,* 5, No.3 (Winter 1979).
2. In his introduction to this poem at Cardiff November 4, 1981 Seamus Heaney acknowledged this flaw. The 1700 years old corpse of a girl from Jutland "made me think of the French collaborators, those girls having their heads shaved, and then of the treatment of 'informers' in Northern Ireland". He sees the poem as "a rebuke to oneself".

3. Heaney comments (Cardiff Reading November 1981) that he was now a full-time writer, living in Wicklow, and looking for exemplars. He was drawn to Mandelstam and "the quality of heroism in his poetry. In a grandiose way I was identifying with Mandelstam".

4. Heaney: "I think that poetry and politics are, in different ways, an articulation, an ordering, a giving of form to inchoate pieties, prejudices, world-views, or whatever. And I think that my own poetry is a kind of slow, obstinate, papish burn, emanating from the ground I was brought up on". "Unhappy and at home." Interview with Seamus Deane, *The Crane Bag*, 1, No. 1.

5. ibid.

6. See later the treatment of spent cartridges in 'The Strand at Lough Beg'.

7. Cardiff Reading: Heaney names Dante as "the poet who has influenced me most over the last ten years. . . . You find everything in him".

8. There are clearly other examples of this type of association in post-war U.K. writing, e.g. Philip Larkin's 'Toads'.

9. This seems notably less contrived than the procession in 'Funeral Rites', *North* p. 16.

10. *Viewpoints*, ed. John Haffenden. Faber 1981, p. 58.

11. ibid. p. 72. S.H. comments: " 'love poems' is a terrible phrase; 'poems about relationships' is a bit limp too perhaps . . . 'Marriage poems', call them. There's no reason why benign emotions shouldn't be able to find utterance"

12. See *Preoccupations*, p. 112. It is used by Yeats as an epigraph in *Explorations*.

13. See Heaney's comments when interviewed by Seamus Deane *Crane Bag*, 1, No. 1. pp. 62-3.

14. See Heaney's comments at the Cardiff Reading November 1981. In his introduction to 'Act of Union' he talked of the map analogy behind that poem. The U.K. mainland as a sexually aroused man—Ireland as a subjugated woman crouching away from him. "A pregnancy poem—male guilt at having started the whole business."

15. 'Yeats as an Example?', *Preoccupations*, p. 112.

16. 'Feeling into Words', *Preoccupations*, p. 60.

17. ibid. p. 113.

18. ibid.

ANNE STEVENSON

The Peace Within Understanding:
Looking at *Preoccupations*

The Peace Within Understanding:
Looking at *Preoccupations*

In an early essay entitled 'The Perfect Critic', T. S. Eliot was at pains to distinguish the practice of criticism from the practice of poetry. Though it is likely, he said, that the poet and the critic will be the same person (since "superior sensibility" is "rare, unpopular and desirable") nevertheless, "the two directions of sensibility are complementary" but distinct. The perfect critic, according to Eliot, must avoid two extremes: over-intellectualization on one hand—because it apes scientific organization—and impressionistic aestheticism on the other. In the early years of this century, critics tended to the latter extreme, and it was primarily at the aesthetic successors of Walter Pater that Eliot directed the admonitions of the first part of his essay. But in recent years twentieth-century critics have leaned in the other direction; so it was with foresight that in Part II of 'The Perfect Critic' Eliot turned his attention to the misuse of emotional and linguistic systematization.

One wonders at this stage what Eliot would have made of Seamus Heaney's *Preoccupations*, which seems to fall into a category Eliot did not anticipate. Heaney's essays are hardly impressionistic in the way Arthur Symons' were. They do not exclaim ecstatically over characters and plots or deliver opinions with regard to the meaning of poetic masterpieces. And yet, all the essays in *Preoccupations* are conspicuously personal. They fall so far short of contemporary standards of "emotional systemization" that we read them as we do Heaney's poems, as distinctive perceptions of a humane, intelligence and eminently generous personality.

It may be that Heaney himself does not consider some of the essays in this book to be "criticism". The memoirs that begin the collection and the moving tribute to Robert Lowell that ends it are personal in the way Heaney's poems are personal—lucid and meticulously fair. Nevertheless, to Eliot, *Preoccupations* might just have verged upon the self-indulgent, since Eliot himself was, as he approvingly wrote of

Swinburne, "one man in his poetry and a different man in his criticism." The intellectual and spiritual strains in Eliot's work proceeded in parallel but distinct lines; indeed, the very stiffness and dryness of his prose seemed to give impetus to the powerful religious intensity of his verse.

We can see right away that Heaney is a poet of an entirely different order, that his poetry and prose are branches of the same tree. The more we read of him, the clearer it becomes how deeply the root of that tree is embedded in the Irish soil of Heaney's childhood. At the same time, neither his poetry or prose appear to be self-indulgent in the way, for instance, Eliot thought Arthur Symons' was. Even Eliot would have agreed, I think, that Heaney's personal impressions rarely make concessions to sentimentality.

Heaney's gift for loving but distanced reminiscence is enhanced by two prevailing preoccupations (the book is well named), one of which it is certain Eliot would have approved. This is Heaney's endemic fascination with language—his imagination which Eliot would have termed "auditory". In his essay on Hughes, Hill and Larkin called 'Englands of the Mind' Heaney uses Eliot's formulation as a touchstone for his own perceptions. But in Heaney (as in Eliot) "auditory imagination" is not only critical terminology; it is a mainspring of his own inspiration. He sees his contemporaries as "living off the hump of English poetic achievement" as he himself draws from the "word-hoard" of the past. What Heaney says about the language of these poets is incisive and true; but by putting their language first, before their meanings or their subject matters, Heaney achieves that distinctively inside perspective on their poetry that a purely academic critic might miss.

The other way in which Heaney eases the burden of his personality has to do with his concern for the emotional and spiritual state of Ireland, and of course, by example of Ireland, for the world itself. Heaney has been criticized—sometimes it seems that he criticizes himself—for not taking sides in The Troubles, for refusing to put a poetic shoulder to the wheel of Irish national sentiment, but instead, opting (more dangerously) for neutrality—as Dante did during the factional fighting in thirteenth/fourteenth century Italy.

Like Dante, Heaney declares an affinity only to peace. Whatever private answers he has made to political criticism, Heaney's considered explanation of his attitude appears consistently and constantly, both in his poetry and in his prose. It is as if it were being more and more fiercely borne in on him just how important peace is to his view of life and of art. In his poems, Heaney writes of peace as Keats—and Wallace Stevens—wrote of beauty, as a state of mind indespensible to creation. The first paragraph of *Preoccupations* is a quotation by way of an epigraph from Yeats's *Explorations* in which Yeats, in turn, quotes from Coventry Patmore: "The end of art is peace." The same inherited quotation appears as a climax in the last verse of 'The Harvest Bow'—among the strongest and most personal poems in *Field Work*.

If, then, we see peace as a condition germane to Heaney's art, and we read his poems and essays in the light of this, we can see how Heaney's sensibility as an artist differs from Eliot's sixty years ago. Heaney's commitment to the art of poetry is no less passionate than Eliot's, but Heaney's is essentially a secular commitment, both in the manner of its language and in its fundamental subjectivity. As Heaney himself declared in an excellent piece of self-analysis written for the *Guardian* in 1972 (*Preoccupations*, p. 34)

> You have to be true to your own sensibility, for faking of feelings is a sin against the imagination. Poetry is out of the quarrel with ourselves and the quarrel with others is rhetoric.

Here, of course, is a case of *Eriger en lois ses impressions personnelles*. For it cannot be said truly that *all* poetry is out of the quarrel with ourselves, only that the kind of poetry Heaney writes is. Heaney's personality and self-conflicts are so central to his perceptions that the abstracting quality Eliot valued (and with equal frankness tended to erect into laws) is sometimes hidden.

This is not to say that either Eliot or Heaney are 'right' in what they claim for art and poetry, but only that they work (or worked) from different principles. In all his criticism and verse, distinguished as it is, Eliot deliberately retreats from himself. He grants us no confidences or personal memoirs. The personal pronoun 'I' is never a focus for the ideas and feelings he presents—although certainly these ideas and feelings have a source in one person's committed, even prejudiced, point of view. Eliot's poetry primarily relates to his preoccupation with language in search of faith; his criticism relates to language in search of objectivity in the discussion of poetry. His strengths, both as a poet and a critic, derive from the objectifying austerity of his intelligence which enabled him to abstract and universalize his feelings without reference to his autobiography. His method was more like that of the Milton he attempted to downgrade than of the Dante he revered.

On a first impression, it looks as if Heaney is closer to Dante in temperament than Eliot was, though of course Heaney is not prone to rehearse the theology of his day in his poems (for theology, substitute science, and we see that Heaney is very different in this respect); nor has Heaney so far engaged in the satisfactory activity of populating Hell with his enemies. Heaney's affinity with Dante, as we might expect, is different from Eliot's. It is Dante's personal predicament that attracts him—Dante's situation in his society (similar to his own) as a scholarly, imaginatively just man who adheres to peace in an environment corrupted by politics and rife with murderous betrayal.

Since Dante is a greater poet—or at least a greater influence in poetry—than any writer of the twentieth century, it is not surprising that Eliot and Heaney have taken from *The Divine Comedy* what respectively they needed to nourish their very different sensibilities. Eliot interpreted Dante's poem as a religious one; Heaney looks to Dante's humanity and sense of justice in the light of his craving for peace. But presumably both poets, in the first instance, responded with excitement to the beauty of Dante's language, and both knew how vital their sense of Dante's art was to their own.

This pillaging of literary precedent is in accordance with Eliot's famous pronouncement with regard to tradition and individual talent; and it also illuminates Heaney's private admission in *Preoccupations* that "the feminine element for me involves the matter of Ireland, and the masculine strain is drawn from the involvement with English literature."

This is a particularly interesting admission, for it is precisely the "feminine" element that is absent from Eliot's criticism. If Heaney's *Preoccupations* represents an advance on the critical dichotomy Eliot so carefully set up and analyzed in 'The Perfect Critic', then Heaney's personal reconciliation between the feminine and masculine sides of his nature is not self-indulgence but a kind of intellectual discovery. It relates closely to the concept we have of intelligence. For if we conceive of intelligence as something distinct from emotion, as Eliot did—if we think of bringing *in* intelligence, as it were, like a schoolmaster to settle a fight between rowdy children, then we miss the subtlety of what intelligences like Heaney's have to teach us. Because Heaney is able to marry intelligence with personal feelings he is able to bring to these essays a wisdom, an understanding that we all recognize but rarely feel free to express.

When the subject becomes an object (as it often does in Heaney's prose) or rather, when that synthesis occurs between subject and object which, familiar to us in poetry, seems somehow forbidden to us in criticism, we automatically fall into the type of thinking of which Eliot's is an example. We separate off and downgrade our emotions (feminine) by 'handling' them with our minds (masculine). I must hastily add that women as well as men habitually adopt a 'masculine' attitude in argument. What I am getting at has nothing to do with what sex we are, but everything to do with what we might call a prejudiced sexualization of ideas over feelings.

It is by overcoming this prejudice, by marrying and balancing intelligence and feeling, that Heaney achieves that warm yet rigorous empathy which enables him—as no other critic I know—to enter into the creative minds of the poets he considers. Naturally, Heaney writes most intimately of poets whose imaginations accord with his own—of Wordsworth, whose voice emerged out of a music overheard in nature and in childhood, and of Patrick Kavanagh, in whom Heaney finds the spiritual father he does not find, really, in Yeats. It is hard to imagine more sympathetic criticism of either of these poets. Yet in both 'The Makings of a Music', which contrasts the speaking voices of Wordsworth and Yeats, and in 'The Sense of Place', in which an illiterate, unconscious (feminine) sense of place is seen, in Kavanagh, to co-exist with a determined (masculine) literary consciousness, Heaney proceeds from questions in his own mind which are central to his personal creative needs.

For all his Irishness, what Heaney seems to be doing in *Preoccupations* is exploring in prose the vein opened up by Robert Lowell in *Life Studies*. After *Life Studies* it seemed possible (perhaps it always was) to break with Eliot, with impersonality, with the stern patriarchal injunction to reduce the female-infected ego—at least in criticism—to invisible pulp. Lowell, under the influence of his psychoanalysis, re-established himself and his life as significant material with which to build, not only a poetry but a literature. Heaney, instinctively breaking the rules banning autobiography and 'self-indulgence', nevertheless understands the advantages of detachment (as Eliot would have understood that term). Rather than shutting out or abandoning the masculine mode of criticism, Heaney brings to it his natural feeling for mystery and divination . . . a femaleness which enriches his poetry to an extent not yet realized, possibly, by the more extreme protagonists of the feminist movement.

Nowhere is the strength of Heaney's androgynous understanding more apparent than in his essay on Gerard Manley Hopkins. Heaney takes as his text the "fire i' the flint" passage from *Timon of Athens*:

> Our poesy is as a gum which oozes
> From whence 'tis nourished: the fire i' the flint
> Shows not till it be struck; our gentle flame
> Provokes itself, and, like the current, flies
> Each bound it chafes.

Predictably, Heaney finds in this passage a parallel between the "gum that oozes" and that "word-hoard" of the embryonic but auditory imagination from which he draws so richly in his poetry. But Heaney is here not so much concerned to explore this home ground of poetic psychology (although he quotes from Eliot, Valéry, Blake and Keats to show the extent of it) as he is to show how Hopkins develops his art out of the other half of Shakespeare's definition. It is from flint that Hopkins strikes his fire, and in contrast to the "oozy marshlight" of symbolism Hopkins's "fretted" and "patterned" masterpiece exudes a masculine brilliance, a command of language which disciplines passion and brings about a music of "deliberating intelligence". Poetry to Keats, says Heaney, has a physical equivalent in the birth pangs of a mother. But Hopkins brings to his craft a siring instinct. "Keats has the life of a swarm, fluent and merged; Hopkins has the design of the honeycomb, definite and loaded. In Keats, the rhythm is narcotic, in Hopkins it is a stimulant to the mind. Keats woos us to receive, Hopkins alerts us to perceive."

Now this is all most enlightening and informative. Heaney's analysis of Hopkins draws on that part of his imagination which gives itself, fluidly and generously, to another poet's reality. Heaney could never have written 'The Wreck of the Deutschland', but he nevertheless sees that it is Hopkins's whole "myth"—a myth, moreover, which "has been lived as the truth by generations before and since Hopkins"—which was lived, too, by Dante and T. S. Eliot, but not, seemingly, by Heaney himself. It is all the more remarkable, therefore, that Heaney so perfectly realizes the "congruence" Hopkins's poetry builds between that poet and his faith, that he sees so clearly that "state of negotiation" (as Ted Hughes has put it) "between the man and his idea of a Creator" without which Hopkins's poetry would never have come into being.

So perhaps the outstanding impression left by this essay, as by most of *Preoccupations*, is of a wise man's liberality which, though personal, is perfectly unselfish. The integrity Heaney brings to his insights is more remarkable (and this is saying a great deal) than the insights themselves. In *Preoccupations* we are given a rare opportunity to explore the creating mind of a brilliant poet who would prefer to let us into the workings of his imagination than to keep us suspiciously at a distance. Heaney's openness is at times frightening; we almost fear for him, for he seems to have no defences—not even a faith.

But perhaps the wise innocence of his penetrating intelligence *is* a sort of faith. As we have seen, Heaney's imagination has been able to draw strength equally from the "hump" of the English literary tradition and from the fecund "bog" of his own and Ireland's history. Out of these conscious and unconscious hemispheres of experience he has constructed a habitable inner world which we may call understanding. The peace Heaney makes for us and himself lies within understanding, even if it may be unachievable in the world outside it. And as for the peace that *passeth* understanding—well that is something Heaney seems, as yet, unprepared to define: Eliot's "still point of the turning world" . . . Dante's "L'Amour che move il sole e l'altre stelle."

CIARAN CARSON

Sweeney Astray: Escaping from Limbo

Sweeney Astray: Escaping from Limbo

"The ruined maid complains in Irish", writes Seamus Heaney in 'Ocean's Love to Ireland' (from *North*), a poem which refers—among other things—to the linguistic colonization of the island. Despite the inexorable erosion of the language over the past few centuries, the ruined maid still complains in Irish: its position as the language of revolution is, for better or worse, enshrined in Sinn Fein's cultural policy; poetry and prose is being written in Irish, largely ignored by students of Irish literature. And if Irish is still alive, however vestigially, the position of English can never be wholly authoritative, as Stephen Dedalus recognises in *A Portrait of the Artist:*

> The language in which we are speaking is his before it is mine. How different are the words *home, Christ, ale, master* on his lips and mine! I cannot speak or write these words without unrest of spirit.

Heaney uses that quotation as preface to his poem 'The Wool Trade', from *Wintering Out,* and the book as a whole is informed by its concerns: take, for example, 'Toome' and 'Broagh', which are playful extensions of the Irish tradition of *dinnsheanchas,* or lore of place-names; or 'The Backward Look':

> A stagger in air
> as if a language
> failed. . .

The language in question is, presumably, Irish, whose ghost is subliminally present throughout the book; this is one way of trying to ease the unrest of the linguistic dilemma which is, to a greater or lesser extent, the heritage of every Irish writer. Joyce invented a language; Beckett wrote in French; others translated, or received their inspiration from translation. We can see how Thomas Kinsella's version of the *Tain,* for example, with its violent narrative, its deep and prophetic utterances, mirrors Kinsella's own work; it is an historical and linguistic imperative. Translation is one way of trying to come to terms with the already created conscience of the Irish language.

So, Seamus Heaney's version of *Buile Suibhne.* Briefly, this is the story of Sweeney, king of Dal Araidhe, who offends the distinguished cleric Ronan Finn, firstly by throwing his psalter into a lake (it is miraculously recovered, unblemished, by an otter), then by killing one of the holy man's acolytes and—worse, perhaps—by throwing his spear at Ronan and denting the sacred bell he wears around his neck. Ronan curses Sweeney on both occasions, prophesying that he will take the form of a bird and eventually die, by the spear. Sweeney goes to fight at the Battle of Moira, and the first part of the malediction is fulfilled. The bulk of the text is taken up by his subsequent peregrinations and hardships, until he is eventually mortally wounded by a spear and reconciled, somewhat unconvincingly, to Christianity.

The story's linguistic embodiment is complex: like many early Irish compositions, it consists of alternate prose and verse, the latter constituting by far the greater part of the work. It might be said that the prose delineates the outward events of the story; the verse recounts an inward, psychological journey; and certainly, much of the effect of the original is gained by this creative interplay. Heaney sees Sweeney as "a figure of the artist, displaced, guilty, assuaging himself of his utterance" (p. viii); he is also the product of the tension between paganism and Christianity, between the natural world and linguistic order. The dialogue is embodied in a significant quibble in the Irish text on the word *eolas,* which Dineen's Irish Dictionary defines variously as "knowledge of direction, way, guidance, bearings; knowledge, learning, skill; a habit, particularly of frequenting a place; a recipe, a prescription or formula; an incantation"; for his part, O'Keefe sometimes renders the word as "home". All these readings are possible: home is where the heart is; it is a state of mind, an incantation. The text is, at times, a catalogue of place-names recited with loving care, all the more so because Sweeney is homeless: it is a significant extension of the *dinnsheanchas* tradition, which existed to give historical legitimacy to territorial claims. A place was not simply a place; it was a story, a history, a creative act, an ordering of time. The ambiguity is seen at its most concise in the lines

cian om eolus-sa
crioch gusa ranag-sa

Unfortunately I cannot give Heaney's version of these lines, since they occur in one of four consecutive stanzas in Section 45 which he omits without acknowledgement.[1] O'Keefe[2] renders them as "far from my home/is the country I have reached", but the matter is more complex. *Cian* means far, both in time and space. For *crioch,* we can take some definitions from a column-long entry in Dineen: "furrow, boundary; limit, end; region, territory; a definite end or object; business; *ceithre criocha deidheanna an duine,* the 'four last things' (death, judgment, heaven, hell)". These meanings are all possible; with the added ambiguity of *eolas,* they combine to give a dense, riddling effect appropriate to Sweeney's state of mind. I do not know if we can call this usage metaphorical; it is, rather, exploitative, the words themselves generating lines of implicit enquiry; or to put it another way, the technique emerges from the "deep structure" of the language. We see the ploy at its most effective in the sixty-five quatrains of Section 40, where the key word *beann* and its oblique forms *binn* and *benn,* together with the adjectival homophone, meaning, "sweet, melodious", occurs no less than forty-three times. Here is Dineen again: "a point, a peak; a crest, a spire; a wing, a branch; a prong; a horn." Again, all these meanings, and others, are played on; their inherent ambiguity represents Sweeney's schizophrenia, his obsession with mountain-tops, antlers, the tops of trees, spears. His original transgression was caused by a spear; so, he will die by the spear. The manic expansion and diminution of his life is summed up in the lines.

> da mbeinn ar gach beinnine
> beinnini ar gach mbenn

A complete translation is impossible. O'Keefe renders this as "If I were on every little point/There would be a pointlet on every point", which sounds pretty silly in English. Heaney glosses it as "I would roost among/Her mazy antlers". What the Irish implies, by its play on the subjunctive of the verb "to be" (da mbeinn), is that the physical world of antlers, mountain-peaks, spears, has become microscopically internalized in a kind of *Third Policeman* logic. The literal world of the noun has become verb. Sweeney himself is not unaware of the play; a few verses later he calls himself *fer benn,* man of the points or peaks, and, by implication, man of being. His is the chronicle of a death foretold; he is living out the knowledge of a prophecy. The intricate circularity of purpose is mirrored in the convention of the Irish verse forms, that they must begin and end on the same word; the effect, at times, is like taking one step forward and two steps back.

With all this in mind, it is no accident that Flann O'Brien used *Buile Suibhne* as an integral part of *At Swim-Two-Birds,* another book about the responsibility of authorship (Sweeney is the author of his own woes, as well as being largely the author of the verse). Or that Heaney himself, in the first poem in the Sweeney section of *Station Island,* should recall his own fascination with writing:

> Take hold of the shaft of the pen.
> Subscribe to the first step taken
> from a justified line
> into the margin.
>
> ('The First Gloss')

The succinctness of those lines is at least partially informed by the poetic method of *Buile Suibhne,* whose basic unit is the "thin small quatrain. . .kind of drills or augers for turning in and they are long and narrow and deep". Eleven different types of quatrain are in fact used in the original, each with its complex set of rules of metre, assonance (or rhyme) and alliteration. Clearly, to attempt an English equivalent is out of the question; even a "literal" translation, with its difficulties of the text's many ambiguities, is a daunting task—and indeed, O'Keefe's English text rarely gives an adequate idea of the hypnotic density of the original:

> O briar, little arched one,
> thou grantest no fair terms,
> thou ceasest not to tear me,
> till thou hast thy fill of blood.
>
> O yew tree, little yew tree,
> in churchyards thou art conspicuous;
> O ivy, little ivy,
> thou art familiar in the dusky wood.
>
> O holly, little sheltering one,
> thou door against wind;
> O ash tree, thou baleful one,
> hand-weapon of a warrior.
>
> O birch, smooth and blessed,
> thou melodious proud one,
> delightful each entwining branch
> in the top of thy crown.

> The aspen a-trembling;
> by turns I hear
> its leaves a-racing —
> meseems 'tis the foray!

In his introduction, Heaney claims that he has "now and again invested the poems with a more subjective tone than they possess in Irish"; this is not entirely true of his rendition of these lines. Granted, the original has a litanic, manic formality; but here, nature is not observed, it is addressed; in their personification, the trees become cyphers for Sweeney's state of mind; nature is internalized. Heaney's descriptive method alters the relationship to that of observer and observed, an attitude that is at once more romantic and less dramatic; it is, perhaps, more meditative:

> Briars curl in sideways,
> arch a stickle back,
> draw blood and curl up innocent
> to sneak the next attack.
>
> The yew tree in each churchyard
> wraps night in its dark hood.
> Ivy is a shadowy
> genius of the wood.
>
> Holly rears its windbreak,
> a door in winter's face;
> life-blood on a spear-shaft
> darkens the grain of ash.
>
> Birch tree, smooth and blessed,
> delicious to the breeze,
> high twigs plait and crown it
> the queen of trees.
>
> The aspen pales
> and whispers, hesitates:
> a thousand frightened scuts
> race in its leaves.

In the original, that last verse reads:

> Crithach ara criothugudh
> atchluinim ma seach

a duille for riothugudh
dar leam as i an chreach

where *crithach* (aspen, or, literally, "shivery" or "shaky") is a near
homophone of *creach* (raid or foray). Heaney's verse necessarily loses
that dramatic ambiguity; but its own aural ambiguity, though
different in emphasis, is appropriate.

The prose, too, has its own difficulties, it is not a merely functional
matter of getting from A to B. The sometimes laconic narrative is
textured by prolix, heavily alliterative word-clumps which reflect the
internal and external action in a kind of playful weightiness. For
example, Section 11:

> . . .rolion nemhain & dobhar & dasacht & faoinnel & fualang &
> folumain & udmhaille, anbsaidhe & anfhaoistine, miosgais gach
> ionaidh ina mbiodh & searc gach ionaidh noco roichedh;
> romheirblighset a meoir, rocriothnaighsiot a chosa, roluathadh a
> chroidhe, roclodhadh a chedfadha, rosaobadh a radharc,
> rotuitset a airm urnocht asa lamhuibh co ndeachaidh la breithir
> Ronain ar gealtacht & ar geinidecht amail gach n-ethaid
> n-aerdha.

O'Keefe gives this as

> and darkness, and fury, and giddiness, and frenzy, and flight,
> unsteadiness, restlessness and unquiet filled him, likewise
> disgust with every place in which he used to be and desire for
> every place which he had not reached. His fingers were palsied,
> his feet trembled, his heart beat quick, his senses were overcome,
> his sight was distorted, his weapons fell naked from his hands, so
> that through Ronan's curse he went, like any bird of the air, in
> madness and imbecility.

Flann O'Brien's version is nearly a parody which nevertheless reflects
the implicit playfulness of the original:

> . . .he was beleagured by an anger and a darkness, and fury and
> fits and frenzy and fright-fraught fear, and he was filled with a
> restless tottering unquiet and with a disgust for all the places that
> he knew and a desire to be where he never was, so that he was
> palsied of hand and foot and eye-mad and heart-quick and went
> from the curse of Ronan bird-quick in craze and madness from
> the battle.

Heaney's method, by contrast, is to overlook the humour and
emphasize the psychological seriousness:

> His brain convulsed,
> his mind split open.
> Vertigo, hysteria, lurchings
> and launchings came over him,
> he staggered and flapped desperately,
> he was revolted by the thought of known places
> and dreamed strange migrations.
> His fingers stiffened,
> his feet scuffled and flurried,
> his heart was startled,
> his senses were mesmerized,
> his sight was bent,
> the weapons fell from his hands
> and he levitated in a frantic cumbersome motion
> like a bird of the air.
> And Ronan's curse was fulfilled.

I suppose this is legitimate, if different in tone to the original; it certainly accords to Heaney's notion of Sweeney as "a figure of the artist, displaced, guilty, assuaging himself by his utterance". I wonder, though, if the original author (or authors) saw it quite like that; there is little evidence of twentieth-century *angst* (or disassociation of sensibility) in the obvious delight in technical virtuousity, or the rigid conventions in which it is achieved. I have noted that Sweeney's schizophrenia is embodied in the Irish text; it is also taken for granted, as is his original violence; these are a necessary part of the story. Certainly, the act of writing is not questioned: that kind of guilt belongs to *Station Island,* and the tension between public and private personae ("You confused evasion and artistic tact", as one of the ghosts is made to say to Heaney). Is *Sweeney Astray* an attempt to assuage another kind of guilt, that of not belonging fully to a linguistic community, whether Irish or English, the "limbo of lost words"?

One of the best poems in *Station Island* is this brief encounter:

Widgeon

> It had been badly shot.
> While he was plucking it,
> he found, he says, the voice box –
>
> like a flute stop
> in the broken windpipe –

and blew upon it
unexpectedly
his own small widgeon cries.

If Sweeney's voice is sometimes that of Heaney, we cannot quibble too much. Until *Sweeney Astray, Buile Suibhne* has lain nearly moribund in the shelves of libraries. No organisation charged with promoting the Irish language has undertaken to make it more easily available. Its resurrection in a new voice can only be commended.

NOTES

1. "Six stanzas have been dropped from Section 16, seven from Section 40 and one from Section 43. . . Section 82 and the first fifteen stanzas of Section 83 have also been excluded." (p. x, *Sweeney Astray*).
2. *Sweeney Astray* is a version based on J.G. O'Keefe's bilingual edition of *Buile Suibhne* (The Frenzy of Sweeney) published by the Irish Texts Society in 1913. The section numbers used here refer to the original text.

BARBARA HARDY

Meeting the Myth: *Station Island*

Meeting the Myth: *Station Island*

Poets arrest drifting passions and ideas and make them parts of a whole rather than disconcerted fragments. Many do so by invoking frameworks of pre-existing mythologies. The resulting relation is as much friction as congeniality, since the fresh talent is necessarily at variance with much that it embraces, because of new times and new personality. An involvement with various myths, pre-Christian, Christian, medieval, Renaissance, Irish and European, has marked Seamus Heaney's poetry from its beginnings in *Death of a Naturalist,* 1966, to the publication of *Sweeney Astray* (his version of the early Irish work *Buile Suibhne*) and *Station Island,* in 1984. Variously and continuously he has used his perception of religious and literary myth in reflecting on personal and political history. Some poets have influenced him as ancestors (Dante, Eliot, Yeats) and some as contemporaries (Hughes, Patrick Kavanagh, Hill). *Station Island* is a very ambitious essay in fortifying and intensifying personal experience through myth.

Station Island has three sections. The first is a group of self-contained lyrics; the second uses a model deriving from St Patrick's Purgatory—also known as Station Island—in Lough Derg, but relies also on Villon and Dante to create testament and purgatory; the third uses the medieval Sweeney as analogue for personal experience, rather as Joyce used Odysseus and Hamlet, Yeats used Cuchulain and Leda, and Eliot used Agamemnon, Ferdinand, and the Fisher King. The three parts are interwoven with common allusions and images, and the most personal poems are often the most mythical. The division defines and differentiates mood and method. The first section deals mostly with the living, the second with the dead, and the third with a blending of the two as the fabulous Sweeney, exiled and distraught, surveys human life—especially art, love, and war—from his birdseye view among the trees. Heaney never loses sight, no matter how far he soaks his poems in myth, of the early Mossbawn landscapes, with their rural images of labour, craft, and nature, and their passions of nostalgia and rejection. What is asserted is self. What is taken from the myths is what is already congenial. This is not the work of negative capability.

The procedures are complex. In a poem called 'Making Strange', Heaney sets up an apparently binary opposition between the unshorn and bewildered peasant, supported by rural simplicities of puddles and stones, and the sophisticated visitor, for whom the old familiar things have to be explained and converted into pastoral. It is a poem about poetic making and reading as well as about past and present. Heaney borrows his title from what the Russian formalist Victor Scklovsky calls defamiliarisation or *ostranenie*. 'Making Strange' is a definition of the poetic process of enlarging and reshaping experience from known particulars. His Muse—understated as "a cunning middle voice"—persuades him to translate the natural world for the travelled stranger by fusing country matters with tradition and symbol:

> Then a cunning middle voice
> came out of the field across the road
> saying, 'Be adept and be dialect,
> tell of this wind coming past the zinc hut,
>
> call me sweetbriar after the rain
> or snowberries cooled in the fog.
> But love the cut of this travelled one
> and call me also the cornfield of Boaz.

The use of "dialect" as adjective, pressing its ambiguity upon us, is part of the strangeness, an adept touch of defamiliarisation. The proposed metaphor cleverly offers its instance of mythical reference, for the cornfield of Boaz doubles allusion by recalling Keats's image of Ruth "in tears amid the alien corn" as well as summoning up harvest generosity, exile, loyalty ("whither thou goest") and renewed love (Ruth's marriage to Boaz). But the poem is not simply a reconstruction of a Biblical scheme, it reaches towards its own parable, and details never thought of in the Bible take on as much metaphorical strength as the allusions. Even the rural facts to be revived in "recitation" are already metaphorical, "in the tubs of his wellingtons" and "in all that keeps pleading and pleading,/these eyes and puddles and stones". The poem is not an instance of estranging and recuperative conjunction, but an allegory. In a different but similarly illustrative way, the title poem in *Death of a Naturalist* is not really about the death of a naturalist. The first term of the contrast, that of the schoolteacher's cosy and superstitious folklore, is no more naturalistic than the adolescent's threatened erotic vision of the frogs as "great slime kings". This is not about the metamorphosis of a naturalist, a scientist or describer of nature, into symbolist, but of the transition from one kind of anthropomorphism to another.

Heaney has been understandably praised for sensuous apprehension of the phenomenal world. But the sensuous early poems about nature, 'Blackberry Picking' for instance, are not simply sensuous. From the beginning, the blackberry remembered is already apprehended as forbidden fruit. The feeling is knowingly adult, sexual and guilty: "its flesh was sweet/Like thickened wine", "summer's blood was in it", and "lust for/Picking". His sensuousness is most frequently translated in metaphor and allegory, rather than through unexplicated metonymies. In this volume, as in the last two or three, the individual sensuous lyric is insistently generalised by analogue and myth.

What one gets from Heaney's Dante, in the 'Station Island' sequence, as from his Bog people, is a new structure for complex experiences of childhood and adolescent recall, an ironic religious sense, and a deep political unease. The new world is rich in images, bright, witty, tender, and rueful, and in ways that are almost entirely expressive of Heaney, not Dante. There is an occasional sense of refreshed traditions, as when Kavanagh rebukes the pilgrim in wry joking tones recalling how lazy Belacqua greets Dante, in purgatory, and mocks his flagging energy. Dante seems to provide a form which is conveniently occupied, rather than a meeting-place which provokes fresh imaginative utterance.

But the drama of purgatorial withdrawal, contemplation, and encounter with alternative selves, is skilfully contrived. The ghosts are given splendid entrances and exits. Two worlds meet in the limbo of reflection when "something came to life in the driving mirror", and the novelist William Carleton crosses from one time to another (II). A girl's image makes a surprise visit, "Where did she arrive from?" (VI). A second cousin's mutilated ghost (recalling Colum McCartney) "trembled like a heatwave and faded" (VII). The disappearance of Joyce's spirit is veiled, as "the downpour loosed its screens round his straight walk" (XII). These transitions are unnerving in wit and ambiguity, imagined for modern and for other worlds. The conversation with ghosts is not Dantean, but a series of personal recollections, recriminations, and confessions. Heaney has no Virgil to guide and interpret, and must face his ghosts head-on, in powerfully particularised images and stories. Sexy and uncanny beasts and flowers are natural and unnatural endearments which invoke the forgotten sweetheart:

> Freckle-face, fox-head, pod of the broom,
> Catkin-pixie, little fern-swish:

(VI)

A simile of drowned and restored construction assembles a monk's face out of vagueness:

> As if the prisms of the kaleidoscope
> I plunged once in a butt of muddied water
> surfaced like a marvellous lightship
>
> and out of its silted crystals a monk's face . . .

(XI)

The image can be shockingly fixed and definite: "I met a young priest, glossy as a blackbird", and "his polished shoes/unexpectedly secular beneath/a pleated, lace-hemmed alb of linen cloth". Memory reduces him to the hard-edged part played in the pilgrim's life, " 'I never could see you on the foreign missions./I could only see you on a bicycle' ". This Section (IV) is a fine compressed piece of complex storytelling. It brings out a contrast between the minor character in someone else's history and the revealed full life, "I lasted/only a couple of years. Bare-breasted/women and rat-ribbed men", "I rotted like a pear". The poet uses congenial images of sex and morbid vegetable life in a sympathetic inventiveness. In Section V, the images from the pastoral matrix turn grotesque: the schoolmaster's adam's apple "worked like the plunger of a pump in drought" in poignant and ludicrous self-parody. The assertion of self can be subtle and sharp, as when the naturalistic simile proposed by the wind-afflatus in 'Making Strange' is used to describe morning smells, "the sex-cut of sweetbriar after rain", with a touch of hot disobedient variation. The image becomes strange rather than familiar, varying the Muse's proposed trope. Early love finds its remarkable narrative poem in VI, where the ambiguity of the women character(s) is just right for the aphrodisiac feelings of deprivation ("As if I knelt for years at a keyhole/Mad for it") and gratified desire. The enlargement of the tiny keyhole of a locked door opens up feelings of tumescence, satisfaction, and generosity matched by gratitude:

> Until that night I saw her honey-skinned
> Shoulder-blades and the wheatlands of her back
> Through the wide keyhole of her keyhole dress
> And a window facing the deep south of luck
> Opened and I inhaled the land of kindness.

Heaney's erotic poetry is very like Hardy's in its enjoyment of details of dress and flesh.

What Dante seems to provide for the 'Station Island' section is a model for a long poem, fragmented but sequential, dislocated but progressive, elastic but shaped, narrative and lyrical, like the form of 'The Waste Land'. Eliot's poem is more reticent than 'Station Island', compressing myth and narration, and using discontinuity to permit and press out moments of sequestered feeling. Heaney's way is to reduce the mythological element, to exploit it structurally rather than narratively, so there are no recuperative lyrical moments like Eliot's conflation of Dante, Bradley, and self, to re-imagine Ugolino in his hunger-tower in 'What The Thunder Said', "I have heard the key/Turn in the door once and turn once only/We think of the key, each in his prison/Thinking of the key".

There are times when Heaney exploits his form of serial vignettes to meet the myth. For instance, suggestions of infernal stasis and purgatorial progress illuminate the historical situation of Northern Ireland. In Section IX the poem dissolves fantastic pilgrimage into a political dream, dreamt "through the black dorm", of the Lough Derg pilgrim's night. The feeling is allowed to be sympathetic without being dangerously partisan. The poet uses his imagination on behalf of a dead terrorist: "Often I was dogs on my own track/Of blood on wet grass that I could have licked". A fragmented elegy speaks of sadness without commitment to a Yeatsian sense, self-doubting though that was, of a terrible beauty in rebellion:

> Unquiet soul, they should have buried you
> In the bog where you threw your first grenade,
> Where only helicopters and curlews
> Make their maimed music . . .

The interruptions of story and image permitted by the dream-poem allow rare statements of a penitential feeling, perhaps too rarely imagined in this purgatory:

'I repent
My unweaned life that kept me competent
To sleepwalk with connivance and mistrust'.

In Section VIII the pilgrim-poet's murdered cousin accuses him of
confusing evasion with artistic tact, and this form is not an evasive
one. It is true that dream permits a romantic recovery from nightmare, "My feet touched bottom and my heart revived". The mood of
affirmation seems to be slyly licensed by the dream play: images of
disgust, "swirl of mucky, glittering flood", are transformed into
another sexy vegetation image, "like a pistil growing from the
polyp", then converted into a religious emblem, "A lighted candle
rose and steadied up". But this poem is the climactic third of a series
of three political poems, all strongly contrasted in manner, if not in
language. They use the baldness of simple speech, " 'Were they in
uniform? Not masked in any way?'" and "'. . .Open up and see
what you have got—pills/or a powder or something in a bottle'",
matter-of-fact narrations and descriptions, and outpourings of praise
and remorse, in ways which are not evasive at all. The political elegy
seems at times to be written by the "young Catholic male"[1]: "There
always was an athlete's cleanliness/shining off him" and "he was still
that same/rangy midfielder in a blue jersey". Remorse is joined with
praise. Poems VII and VIII are stories which confess the pilgrim's
"timid circumspect involvement", and rebuke his evasion through
poetry, "you whitewashed ugliness and drew/the lovely blinds of the
Purgatorio". After this stunning piece of reflexive writing, it is not
surprising that it takes a dream to raise the religious symbol and
dissolve nightmare. But the relief of waking is not the end of poem IX.
There is a final lapse of self-hatred in which the pilgrim criticises his
own "biddability", then moves into an ambiguous and ironic
affirmation:

> Then I thought of the tribe whose dances never fail
> For they keep dancing till they sight the deer.

(IX)

The most willed and unimaginative sections of 'Station Island'
seem to be those invoking other authors—Carleton, Kavanagh, and
Joyce—where poetic passions are more sluggish than those in the
pastoral and political poetry. Ancestors and peers are barely
represented. Once again, the second term of a pairing is occupied

rather than characterised. One has only to recall Auden's appreciative invocations of "black Tennyson", in *New Year Letter,* or the Freud, Pascal and Henry James of his character-poems, to see where Heaney's strength does not lie, or is not yet shown. Compared with these, let alone with Dante's bitter characterisations, his portraits are imaginary rather than imaginative. For anyone who does not know Carleton there is no vividness in section II. Joyce's voice is beautifully described as "eddying with the vowels of all rivers", and called "cunning, narcotic, mimic, definite" (XII), but the language and feeling spoken for him are not Joycean. His counselling words are definite, but not cunning, narcotic or mimic. There is another literary poem in the first section, 'The Birthplace', where Hardy is invoked in a similarly shadowy and obvious fashion, and where the strongest part of the poem, a reticent sexual anecdote, is much more interesting than anything about the birthplace, where some of the details don't even ring true. To see in a single bed "a dream of discipline" seems to neglect our knowledge of Hardy's tormented sexuality. Once more, Heaney calls to other images in order to have his say, not to make them strangely familiar or familiarly strange through meeting opposition and difference. This is domination, not discovery.

The last section, 'Sweeney Redivivus' is also vulnerable to the charge that Heaney tends to occupy convenient and congenial corners of large tragic myths. In an interview recorded for the BBC *Kaleidoscope* programme (11-10-84), he made the disarming admission that he chooses Sweeney for his rhyme with Heaney, explaining that he wasn't driven mad, though he did move to exile among the trees of Wicklow. Sweeney's madness and wildness are powerful elements in the mediaeval poem and though these "glosses", as Heaney calls them, are confessedly imagined "in contexts far removed from early medieval Ireland", many of them are resolved meditations on childhood, art and politics, harking back to familiar feelings and only loosely responsive to the Sweeney themes. 'Holly', for instance, is an intensely physical lyric about the outside and inside worlds of nature and domesticity which simply reminds us of the prevailing theme by its tree-image, and the specific reference to "holly", one of Sweeney's trees. It invokes exposure to the natural world which Heaney rightly praises in early Irish poetry and in Shakespeare's Poor Tom, but is as much about enclosure, ending in a yearning for the defensiveness of a book's "glittering shield-wall". 'In the Chestnut Tree' is one of Heaney's rare contemplative lyrics about the natural world, which celebrates a resilient old tree tenderly, humorously, admiringly, and precisely. It gives a terrifying glimpse of death, little but persistent, from the vantage point of vitality:

> And the little bird of death
> piping and piping somewhere
>
> in her gorgeous tackling? Surely not.
> She breathes deep and stirs up the algae.

Sweeney may have helped to make the poem, but has been discarded. Another tree poem, 'In the Beech', begins as a bitter pastoral, re-calling a childhood sex-nest and shelter, "where the school-leaver discovered peace/to touch himself in the reek of churned-up mud", which is also a post from which he looks out at the planes and tanks of World War II. Its conclusion seems to edge away from irony towards secure, deep-rooted, and tender celebration:

> My hidebound boundary tree. My tree of knowledge.
> My thick-tapped, soft-fledged, airy listening post.

Once more, Heaney converts wildness into mildness, exposure into shelter, doubleness into simplicity. The myth's depths are not tapped.

Yeats used the mask or the image to summon opposition. Heaney uses the Sweeney rhyme to assert and re-assert the securities of personal experience, neglecting Sweeney's violence and unease. In the *Kaleidoscope* interview I have mentioned Heaney said he thought of himself as belonging to the North, but felt at ease everywhere in Ireland, "in it or out of it". In *Buile Suibhne* Sweeney's transformation into half-beast is a punishment for sacrilege and aggression, imagined as a state of acute unease, nakedness, exile and madness. The religion, geography, and exile are relevant themes but Heaney's passions are usually, though not always, less destructive. His penances (which include having to translate St John of the Cross,[2] which seems more like a grace than a penance) come out quietly, and are often rationally resolved.

In 'The First Kingdom', for instance, Heaney is imagining exile, but from a first and familiar kingdom, backward-looking, easily hier-archical, where "the nobles/lorded it over the hindquarters of cattle". His exile is that of growth, maturity, detachment, expressed in rational critique:

> They were two-faced and accommodating.
> And seed, breed and generation still

> they are holding on, every bit
> as pious and exacting and demeaned.

It's a good poem, but seems to have little to do with the presiding myth. Another poem, 'Sweeney's Returns', is a finely imagined poem of startled deprivation, recalling mad Sweeney's return to his wife Eovann. The mythological bird-image produces imagery of precariousness and exclusion, "I perched on the sill", and of distraction, "I floundered/in my wild reflection in the mirror". Once more, this is to meet the myth in one small corner, where loss and absence is familiarly imaged, not re-imagined, through Heaney's typical warm sense of domestic object, "a bangle/lay in the sun", "the tucked and level bed", and erotic flower, "the fleshed hyacinth".

Heaney's meditations on the Sweeney figure are rooted in Mossbawn. His collection of essays and reviews, *Preoccupations. Selected Prose 1968-78,* includes an essay on early Irish nature poetry, called 'The God in the Tree', which anticipates the preface to *Sweeney Astray,* in its praise of early Celtic nature poetry for its representation of "the sharp tooth of winter". He quotes Sweeney's praise of trees, which is a congenial source for the flora of his own tree poems. Here too, he picks significantly on the assonance, not the dissonance, linking him with Sweeney, king-poet-exile, "another wood-lover and a tree-hugger, a picker of herbs and drinker from wells". He praises Sweeney's poetry of praise. He stresses its exposure to "nature's abundance", not its cruelty. He identifies with its love and affirmation, not its aggression, pains, and madness.

In the essay 'Mossbawn', he describes the forbidden ground of bog and moss haunted by Tom Tipping, whose name became "synonymous with mystery man", like the family of tinkers, also called Sweeney, who used to camp in the ditchbacks described in *Sweeney Astray.* Such figures inhabit "the realm of bogeys", and are part of a dangerous field of force, "mankeepers and mosscheepers, creatures uncatalogued by any naturalist, but none the less real for that". The childhood bogey grew up into myth. Experience became literary, joining Irish and English mythology[3] and poetry. The poem 'The King of the Ditchbacks', a Sweeney-like poem outside the Sweeney section, concludes the first group of lyrics. Like *Buile Suibhne* it is written in verse and prose and uses myth to face fear, destructiveness, and mystery. The poet contemplates an unnamed *alter ego,* a signaller, opening a "dark morse", connected with obsessive and deadly night fears ("Are you the one I ran upstairs to find drowned under running water in the bath?"), identified as hunted, "my stealth was second nature'', and as hunter. The speaker is finally initiated, in rites which bring him close to beasts and trees, and in primitive camouflage:

> they dressed my head in a fishnet
> and plaited leafy twigs through meshes

He is like a bird, ''my vision was a bird's/at the heart of a thicket'', invited to a hunt, '' 'Come back to us . . . when we hide in the stooked corn/when the gundogs can hardly retrieve/what's brought down' '', and finally resolved, in the New Testament image of the rich young man who left ''everything he had/for a migrant solitude'', at least in Heaney's story. Both the complicity and the privacy are intensely imagined.

One can see the elements of personal allegory, but the poem transcends these. The rich young man returns again, in one of many subterranean movements in a volume which brings poems together in ways both connective and corrective. The very last of the 'Sweeney Redivivus' poems, 'On the Road', joins Dante's ''seraph-haunted'' landscape with the tourist driving in the Dordogne. It repeats the young man's question, ''*what must I do to be saved?*'' and concludes not with a response to Christ's, ''*Sell all you have/and give to the poor*'', but with a pre-Christian image, not of moral action, but of contemplation and art. His hunt finds an aesthetic, not a kinetic, quarry, in a cave where the deer is cut into rock, to be gazed on:

> until the long dumbfounded
> spirit broke cover
> to raise a dust
> in the font of exhaustion.

That perfected oxymoron makes an imaginatively open ending: dust instead of water for a new christening, a sense of exhaustion and vitality wrung from ambiguity and wit, in ''broke cover'' and ''raise a dust''. These two poems still show Heaney asserting himself, using Dante, Sweeney, Christ and primitive art for personal allegory, but with a passionate, dedicated, and ironic sense of Sweeney's iconoclasm and exile. Sweeney is mixed with Dante, to create the eclecticism and openness of the last sequence, and to tighten the forms of the volume as a whole.

One of the most impressive and difficult of these poems is 'Sandstone Keepsake'. It is typical of the poet's praise of the world of things, domestic (flat iron), rural, literary (a chip off Joyce's tower), historic, manmade, picked up at random from the earth's face. (It is carefully placed before a sequence of object-poems called 'Shelf-Life'.) It is a poem about the poet's sense of wonder and detachment, as he dares to contemplate the natural world at the frontier where history and politics overlook solitary meditation. It is also a poem about a bondage to history. The "I" of the poem is called "one of the venerators". On a first reading[4] the poem seems to be about a dared act of veneration, focussed and illustrated by the stone, contemplated at a time removed from the moment of its discovery and remembered at that moment: "It is a kind of chalky russett", "It was ruddier, with an underwater/hint of contusion". What the keepsake memorialises—so the first reading may go—is the contrast between a detached and quietist veneration of this ancient object, picked up in a lough which separates the Republic of Ireland from Northern Ireland and the political world of civil war and rebellion. The speaker sees the internment camp in County Derry, from his "free state of image and allusion" in Donegal, across the border. The individual vision cannot exclude history from the landscape. The trained binoculars spot him, then discard his unimportant and unthreatening image. But to be seen seeing changes the act of seeing and forces a recognition of an uncertainty principle. He is

> a silhouette not worth bothering about,
> out for the evening in scarf and waders
> and not about to set times wrong or right,
> stooping along, one of the venerators.

The first reading may be halted by that "free" state of allusion. The innocence of the innocent stone is first unsettled by the "hint of contusion", a quiet poetic signal. Then the object is pulled into a mythological field of force, contemplated as "a stone from Phlegethon,/bloodied on the bed of hell's hot river". This immediately follows an image of lights coming on "round the perimeter/of the camp", which announces boundary, threat, and embattled occupation. The object loses its innocence, but its sophistication is not fully intelligible unless we know or until we get to know the next reference and elaboration, which makes the classical river meet the Dantean myth. (Another instance of the way these poems break the bounds of sections.) The poet uses the sensation of seeing his hand steam ("smoke") in the cold air to introduce a victim from the *Inferno*.

He feels as if he had plucked the heart "that damned Guy de Montfort to the boiling flood". The transformation is permitted by the colour, shape, and size of the stone as well as the steaming hand, though it is detached, if not undone, by the words "but not really". The most difficult detail, which many readers will need to look up, comes as the speaker remembers the heart of Guy's victim "in its casket, long venerated". Heaney's note here is puzzlingly incomplete, referring us to Dorothy Sayers' note in the Penguin translation of Dante in almost as many words as could have said that the heart of Henry, son of Richard, Duke of Cornwall, nephew of Henry III, was supposed to have been contained in a casket or held in the hand of his statue, on London Bridge. Henry was killed by Guy de Montfort at High Mass in a church at Viterbo, in an act of revenge. The full implications of veneration utterly destroy the innocence of the stone, and complicate the conclusion. Veneration is made political and contemplation is implicated in history. The "free" image is bound to history by association with a national and military memorial to a victim of sacrilegious revenge: the murderer's father was killed at the Battle of Evesham in a civil war. Guy is one of the spirits who were "violent against their neighbours" (*Inferno,* Canto XII).

The sly use of "free" indirect style which attributes the final "one of the venerators" both to the indifferent dismissal by the watchtowers of the English camp, and to the speaker's rueful recognition, deepens the irony. The poem asks a question about veneration, perhaps several questions: is the camp across the border right to write off veneration? is it possible to pick up a stone and simply wonder? are keepsakes arbitrary? can the poet meditate, praise, remember, and look without being political? how is the innocent eye implicated in history?

The poem's allusiveness, and the poet's elusive gloss, force a sequence of two readings or stages of reading. The second contains the opposition of two irreconcilable views. The poem becomes loaded, but not by accretion, but by contradiction. The reader loses innocence, like the stone and the venerator. One meaning goes against the grain of the other, and the reader's response is most subtly shifted and acknowleged by the poem. The metaphor "hint" uses the rhetoric of hinting. The metaphor "free state of image" questions the possibility of free art or language in Ireland or poetry. Its allusion to "allusion" prompts a weighing-up of ways in which myth works, a contemplation of its enlargements and deconstructions.

The sense of the poem as clandestine is compounded by Heaney's own comments in that *Kaleidoscope* programme (which excerpted the last stanza). The poet identified himself with the simple interpretation of my proposed first reading, as if the myth and the allusion didn't exist. Poems move out of the poet's control, if they are good enough. The poem knows more than the poet. This poem is honestly untrustworthy. It is a *de facto* solution to Heaney's anxieties about poetic feeling and history and his fears of blandness, propaganda, and complicity. It demonstrates the impossibility of naturalistic and poetic quietism in an unquiet state. The enlargement and friction of myth is psychically rich and historically unnerving.

NOTES

1. Seamus Deane, '"Unhappy and at Home"', Interview with Seamus Heaney', *The Crane Bag,* I, No.1 (Spring 1977).
2. Heaney's reasons for choosing to translate 'Cantar del alma que se heulga de concoscer a Dios por fe' may be its lack of mysticism, its didacticism, appropriate to the Monk's function and purpose, and its combination of Spanish with Italian metres. His fine ear makes it a translation which sounds closer to the original rhythms than that of Roy Campbell's more literal version. One of Heaney's several deviations, which include a puzzling reversal of stanzas 5 and 6, is the introduction of "repining" in the last stanza, with its sense of loss and remorse which is apt for Heaney but not for St John. I am grateful to Professor A I Watson, of the Spanish Department, Birkbeck, for reading the original poem with me, and making most of these suggestions.
3. In this essay, the reprinted essay on 'The God in the Tree', and in the Introduction to *Sweeney Astray,* there are brief references to bogeys, 'mystery man', Poor Tom, and *Sir Gawain and the Green Knight.* In *Sweeney Astray,* Heaney says, rather obscurely, that Sweeney is "not a given figure of myth or legend". He is, however, closely related to the wodwo or savage man of myth, legend, and many literatures. The classic text on the subject, as interesting to a study of these Sweeney poems as Jessie Weston's *From Ritual to Romance* is for 'The Waste Land', is Richard Bernheimer's *Wild Men in the Middle Ages* (Harvard University Press, 1952).
4. I am grateful to the following first-year English students at Birkbeck for their concentrated reading and discussion of this poem: Deborah Fenn, Anne Power, John Russell, John Smyrniotis, and Doreen Wainwright.

BIBLIOGRAPHY

Bibliography

Works by Seamus Heaney

Death of a Naturalist. London: Faber, 1966.
Door into the Dark. London: Faber, 1969.
Wintering Out. London: Faber, 1972. New York: Oxford University Press, 1972.
Stations. Belfast: Ulsterman Publications, 1975.
North. London: Faber, 1975. New York: Oxford University Press, 1976.
Field Work. London: Faber, 1979. New York: Farrar, Straus, Giroux, 1979.
Selected Poems 1965-1975. London: Faber, 1980. New York: Farrar, Straus, Giroux, 1980.
Preoccupations: Selected Prose 1968-1978. London: Faber, 1980. New York: Farrar, Straus, Giroux, 1980.
An Open Letter. Derry: Field Day Theatre Pamphlets, 1983.
Sweeney Astray. London: Faber, 1984. New York: Farrar, Straus, Giroux, 1984.
Station Island. London: Faber, 1984. New York: Farrar, Straus, Giroux, 1984.
'Among Schoolchildren': A John Malone Memorial Lecture. Belfast, University, 1984.
Hailstones. Dublin: Gallery Press, 1985.

Interviews

'Le Clivage Traditionnel' (anon.). *Les Lettres Nouvelles,* (March 1973), pp. 87-9.
Interview (Harriet Cooke). *Irish Times,* 28 December 1973, p. 8.
'Unhappy and at Home' (Seamus Deane). *The Crane Bag,* 1 No. 1 (1977), pp. 61-7.
'Talk with Seamus Heaney' (Seamus Deane). *New York Times Review,* 84 No. 48 (1979), pp. 79-101.
'Raindrop on a Thorn: Interview with Seamus Heaney' (R. Druce). *Dutch Quarterly Review,* 9 No. 1 (1979), pp. 45-6.
'Poets on Poetry' (Patrick Garland). *The Listener,* 8 November 1973, p. 629.

'Meeting Seamus Heaney: An Interview' (John Haffenden). *London Maga-zine,* vol. 19 (June 1979), pp. 5-28.
'An Interview with Seamus Heaney' (James Randall). *Ploughshares,* 5 No. 3 (1979), pp. 7-22.
'The Sunday Interview' (Caroline Walsh). *Irish Times,* 6 December 1975, p. 5.
'An Interview with Seamus Heaney' (Frank Kinahan). *Critical Inquiry,* Spring 1982, pp. 405-414.

Critical Works on Seamus Heaney

Alvarez, A. 'A Fine Way with Language'. *New York Review of Books,* 6 March 1980, pp. 16-7.
Anon. 'Fear in a Tinful of Bait'. *The Times Literary Supplement,* 17 July 1969, p. 770.
Anon. 'Semaphores of Hurt'. *The Times Literary Supplement,* 15 December 1972, p. 1524.
Anon. 'Seamus Heaney'. *Literary Review,* vol. 22 (Winter 1979), pp. 210-11.
Anon. 'Ulsterman who became a Poet by Accident'. *Ulster Commentary,* No. 353 (February 1976) p. 8.
Bailey, Anthony. 'A Gift for Being in Touch'. *Quest,* January/February 1978, pp. 38-46, 92-3.
Beer, Patricia. 'Seamus Heaney's Third Book of Poems'. *The Listener,* 7 December 1972, p. 795.
Beford, William. 'To Set the Darkness Echoing'. *Delta,* No. 56 (1977), pp. 2-7.
Begley, Marie. 'The North: Silent Awareness with Seamus Heaney', from *Rambles in Ireland,* Devin-Adair, 1977.
Berke, Roberta. *Bounds out of Rounds.* Oxford: Oxford University Press, 1982.
Bloom, Harold. 'The Voice of Kinship'. *The Times Literary Supplement,* 8 February 1980, pp. 137-8.
Brinton, George A. 'A Note on Seamus Heaney's *Door into the Dark'.* Con-temporary Poetry, 1, No. 2 (1973), pp. 30-4.
Brown, Maey P. 'Seamus Heaney and *North'. Studies: An Irish Quarterly Review,* LXX Winter, 1981, pp. 289-296.
Brown, Terrence. *Northern Voices. Poets from Ulster.* Dublin: Gill & Macmillan, 1975.
Browne, Joseph. 'Violent Prophecies: The Winter and Northern Ireland'. *Eire-Ireland,* 10, No. 2 (Summer 1975), pp. 109-119.
Buttel, Robert. *Seamus Heaney.* Lewisburg Pa.: Bucknell University Press, 1975.
Carson, Ciaran. 'Escaped from the Massacre?'. *The Honest Ulsterman,* 50 (Winter 1975), pp. 183-6.
Curtis, Simon. 'Seamus Heaney's *North'. Critical Quarterly,* vol. 16 (Spring 1974), pp. 35-48.

Curtis, Tony. 'A More Social Voice: Seamus Heaney's *Field Work'. Poetry Wales,* 16, No. 3 (1981), pp. 79-101.

Curtis, Tony. *Station Island. Poetry Wales,* 20, No. 3 (1985), pp. 91-95.

Donoghue, Denis. Review of *Field Work. New York Times Book Review,* 2 December 1979, pp. 1 & 45-6.

Dunn, Douglas. ed *Two Decades of Irish Writing.* Manchester: Carcanet Press, 1975, Chester Springs, Pa: Dufour Editions Inc., 1975.

Dunn, Douglas. 'Manana is Now'. *Encounter,* November 1975, pp. 76-81.

Ehrenpreis, Irvin. 'Digging In'. *New York Review of Books,* 8 October 1981, pp. 45-6.

Fitzgerald, Robert. 'Seamus Heaney: an appreciation'. *New Republic,* No. 174 (27 March 1976), pp. 27-9.

Foster, John Wilson. 'The Poetry of Seamus Heaney'. *Critical Quarterly,* vol. 16, (Spring 1974), pp. 35-48.

Foster, John Wilson. 'Seamus Heaney's "A Lough Neagh sequence": sources and motifs'. *Eire-Ireland,* 12, No. 2 (Summer 1977), pp. 138-42.

Gitzen, Julian. 'British Nature Poetry Now'. *Midwest Quarterly,* 15, No. 4 (Summer 1974), pp. 323-7.

Gitzen, Julian. 'An Irish Imagist'. *Studies in the Humanities,* 4, No. 2 (1975), pp. 10-13.

Grant, Damian. 'Verbal Events'. *Critical Quarterly,* vol. 16 (Spring 1974), pp. 81-86.

Green, Carlanda. 'The Feminine Principle in Seamus Heaney's Poetry'. *Ariel,* July 1983, pp. 3-13.

Hederman, M. P. 'Seamus Heaney: the reluctant poet'. *Crane Bag,* 3, No. 2 (1979), pp. 61-70.

Hooker, Jeremy. 'Seamus Heaney's *North'. The Poetry of Place,* Manchester: Carcanet, 1982, pp. 71-4.

Johnston, Dillan. 'The Enabling Ritual: Irish Poetry in the Seventies'. *Shenandoah,* 25, No. 4 (Summer 1974), pp. 3-24.

Kiely, Benedict. 'A Raid into Dark Corners: the Poems of Seamus Heaney'. *The Hollins Critic,* vol. 4 (4 October 1970), pp. 1-12.

King, P. R. 'I See Through Origins'. *Nine Contemporary Poets,* London: Methuen, 1979, pp. 190-219.

Liddy, James. 'Ulster Poets and the Catholic Muse'. *Eire-Ireland,* 13, No. 4 (Winter 1978), pp. 126-37.

Lloyd, D. 'The Two Voices of Seamus Heaney's *North'. Ariel,* vol. 10 (October 1979), pp. 5-13.

Longley, Edna. 'Fire and Air'. *The Honest Ulsterman,* 50 (Winter 1975), pp. 179-83.

Longley, Edna. 'Stars and Horses, Pigs and Trees'. *Crane Bag,* 3, No. 2 (1979), pp. 54-60.

Longley, Edna. 'Heaney: Poet as Critic'. *Fortnight,* December 1980, pp. 15-16.

Longley, Michael. 'Poetry'. In Michael Longley (ed.), *Causeway: The Arts in Ulster*, Belfast: Arts Council of Northern Ireland, 1971, pp. 95-109.

Mahon, Derek. 'Poetry in Northern Ireland'. *Twentieth Century Studies*, November 1970, pp. 89-93.

Maxwell, D. E. S. 'Imagining the North: violence and the Writers'. *Eire-Ireland*, 8, No. 2 (Summer 1973), pp. 91-107.

McGuiness, Arthur E. ' "Hoarder of the common ground": tradition and ritual in Seamus Heaney's poetry'. *Eire-Ireland*, 13, No. 2 (Summer 1978), pp. 71-82.

McGuiness, Arthur E. 'The Craft of Diction: Revision in Seamus Heaney's Poems'. In Maurice Harmon (ed.) *Image and Illusion: Anglo-Irish Literature and its Contexts*, Portmarnock, Co. Dublin: Wolfhound Press, 1979, pp. 62-91.
    also in *Irish University Review*, 9, No. 1 (1979), pp. 62-91.

Miller, Karl. 'Opinion'. *The Review*, 27, No. 8 (Autumn/Winter 1971-2), pp. 41-52.

Montague, John. 'Order in Donnybrook Fair'. *The Times Literary Supplement*, 17 November 1972, p. 313.

Morrison, Blake. 'Out from the School'. *New Statesman*, 9 November 1979, pp. 722-3.

Morrison, Blake. 'Speech and Reticence: Seamus Heaney's *North*'. In Jones and Schmidt (eds.) *British Poetry since 1970: a Critical Survey*, Manchester: Carcanet Press, 1980, pp. 103-111.

Morrison, Blake. *Seamus Heaney*. London: Methuen, 1982.

Morrison, Blake. ' "Encounters with Familiar Ghosts": *Station Island* and *Sweeney Astray*'. *Times Literary Supplement*, 19th October, 1984, pp. 1191-92.

Mullan, Fiona. 'Seamus Heaney: The Poetry of Opinion'. *Verse*, 1 (1984), pp. 15-22.

Murphy, Richard. 'Poetry and Terror'. *New York Review of Books*, 30 September 1976, pp. 38-40.

O'Brien, Conor Cruise. 'A Slow North-East Wind'. *The Listener*, 25 September 1975, pp. 404-5.

O'Brien, Darcy. 'Seamus Heaney and Wordsworth: A Correspondent Breeze'. In *The Nature of Identity: Essays Presented to Donald E. Hayden by the Graduate Faculty of Modern Letters, The University of Tulsa*, The University of Tulsa, 1981, pp. 37-46.

Parini, J. 'Seamus Heaney: the Ground Possessed'. *Southern Review*, vol. 16 (Winter 1980), pp. 100-123.

Pearson, Henry. 'Seamus Heaney: A Bibliographical Checklist'. *American Book Collector*, III, March/April, 1982, pp. 31-42.

Quinlan, Kieran. 'Unearthing a Terrible Beauty: Seamus Heaney's Victims of Violence'. *World Literature*, Summer, 1983, pp. 365-69.

Redshaw, Thomas D. ' "Ri" as in Regional: Three Ulster Poets'. *Eire-Ireland*, 9, No. 2 (Summer 1974), pp. 41-64.

Ricks, Christopher. 'Lasting Things'. *The Listener*, 26 June 1969, pp. 900-1.

Ricks, Christopher. 'The Mouth, the Meal, the Book'. *London Review of Books*, 8 November 1979, pp. 4-5.

Riddell, Alan. 'Poet of Divided Ireland'. *Daily Telegraph*, 14 February 1976, p. 14.

Schirmer, G. A. 'Seamus Heaney: Salvation in Surrender'. *Eire-Ireland*, 15, No. 4 (Winter 1980), pp. 139-46.

Sharratt, Bernard. 'Memories of Dying: the Poetry of Seamus Heaney'. *New Blackfriars*, vol. 57 (July 1976), pp. 313-21, and vol. 57 (August 1976), pp. 364-77.

Silkin, Jon. 'Bedding the Locale'. *New Blackfriars*, vol. 54 (March 1973), pp. 130-3.

Silverlight, John, 'Brooding Images'. *The Observer*, 11 November 1979, p. 37.

Stallworthy, Jon. 'The Poet as Archaeologist: W.B. Yeats and Seamus Heaney'. *The Review of English Studies*, XXXIII, No. 130, 1982, pp. 158-74.

Stevenson, Anne. 'Letter: Seamus Heaney'. *The Times Literary Supplement*, No. 4013 (1980), p. 208.

Thwaite, Anthony. 'Neighbourly Murders'. *The Times Literary Supplement*, 1 August 1975, p. 866.

Thwaite, Anthony. 'The Hiding Place of Power'. *The Times Literary Supplement*, 31 October 1980, p. 1222.

Vendler, Helen. 'The Music of What Happens'. *The New Yorker*, 28 September 1981, pp. 146-57.

Waterman, Andrew. 'Ulsterectomy'. In Dannie Abse (ed.) *Best of the Poetry Year* 6, London: Robson, 1979, pp. 42-57.

Zoutenbi, R. 'The Matter of Ireland and the Poetry of Seamus Heaney'. *Dutch Quarterly*, 9, No. 1 (1979), pp. 4-23.

INDEX TO POEMS
AND ESSAYS DISCUSSED

Index to Poems and Essays Discussed

Notes on Contributors

Tony Curtis is Senior Lecturer in English at the Polytechnic of Wales. He has written a critical introduction to the work of Dannie Abse in the Writers of Wales Series, and is presently editing a collection of essays, *Wales: The Imagined Nation* for Poetry Wales Press. He has published and broadcast widely on both sides of the Atlantic and his poetry has won a number of honours including, an Eric Gregory Award in 1972 and the Welsh Arts Council's Young Poets Prize in 1974. In 1984 he was the winner of the National Poetry Competition. His most recent collection of poems is *Letting Go* (Poetry Wales Press, 1983).

Roland Mathias is a full-time writer. He took a first in Modern History at Oxford in 1936, then B. Litt. and M.A. degrees. Formerly Headmaster of King Edward's Five Ways School in Birmingham, he was also editor of the *Anglo-Welsh Review* for many years. He has published on David Jones, Dylan Thomas and most aspects of Anglo-Welsh literature. A notable poet, he was awarded the Welsh Arts Council's Prize in 1969. His collected essays on Anglo-Welsh literature, *A Ride Through the Wood,* are published in 1985 by Poetry Wales Press.

Dick Davis is also a full-time writer, who has had three collections of poetry published by the Anvil Press. His reviews and articles appear in the best U.K. journals, and his full-length study of Ivor Winters was published by the University of Georgia Press in 1982. He is a Fellow of the Royal Society of Literature.

Philip Hobsbaum is Reader in English at Glasgow University. A founder member of The Group in London during the fifties and sixties, Dr. Hobsbaum has published six collections of poetry including *Coming Out Fighting* and *In Retreat* (Dufour Editions) and is the author of Reader's Guides to Dickens and Lawrence. His recent critical book was *Tradition and Experiment in English Poetry*. Philip Hobsbaum taught Seamus Heaney at Queen's University, Belfast, and is acknowledged by Heaney as one of the prime influences on his work in the essay 'Belfast' in *Preoccupations*.

Anne Stevenson was born in Vermont. Her first two collections of poetry were published by the Wesleyan University Press, but five subsequent books have appeared from O.U.P. in England. A regular contributor to the *T.L.S.* and other leading journals, she has been Writer in Residence at the University of Newcastle. Her new collection, The Fiction-Makers is a 1985 Poetry Book Society Choice selection.

Edna Longley is a Lecturer in English at Queen's University, Belfast. Her criticism and reviews are widely published. In 1973 she edited the standard edition of Edward Thomas's poetry, and in 1981 his selected prose, *A Language not to be Betrayed.*

Ciaran Carson worked as a civil servant and as a teacher before becoming Traditional Arts Officer at the Arts Council of Northern Ireland. He was born in Belfast and educated at Queen's University there. Although his first language is Irish he has published a collection of poems in English, *The New Estate,* with Belfast's Blackstaff Press, and writes a regular traditional music column for *The Belfast Review.*

Barbara Hardy is Professor of English at Birkbeck College, University of London, and Visiting Lecturer at a number of universities including Northwestern, Princeton, Dijon and Stockholm. A leading literary critic and reviewer, she also writes poetry. Her publications include: *The Novels of George Eliot, The Moral Art of Dickens, The Advantage of the Lyric,* and, most recently, *Forms of Feeling in Victorian Fiction.*